ALMA HITCHCOCK

THE WOMAN BEHIND THE MAN

ALMA HITCHCOCK

THE WOMAN BEHIND THE MAN

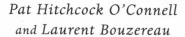

Pat Hitchcock O'Connell
and Laurent Bouzereau

BERKLEY BOOKS, NEW YORK

B

A Berkley Book
Published by The Berkley Publishing Group
A division of Penguin Group (USA) Inc.
375 Hudson Street
New York, New York 10014

Printing History
Berkley hardcover edition / May 2003

Library of Congress Cataloging-in-Publication Data
O'Connell, Pat Hitchcock
    Alma Hitchcock: the woman behind the man / Pat
Hitchcock O'Connell and Laurent Bouzereau.
    p.   cm.
    ISBN: 0-425-19005-6
    Includes bibliographical references.
    1. Reville, Alma. 2. Hitchcock, Alfred, 1899—
    Marriage. 3. Screenwriters—United States—
    Biography. I. Title.
PS3535.E86 Z68 2003
822' .912—dc21   2003043722

Printed in the United States of America
10 9 8 7 6 5 4 3 2 1

This book is lovingly dedicated to

my daughters, Mary, Tere, and Katie,
my sons-in-laws, Jerry, Paul, and Bruce
and
my grandchildren, Melissa, Kelly, Caitlin, Trisha, Kate,
Samantha, and Christopher

CONTENTS

ACKNOWLEDGMENTS

THE AUTHORS WOULD like to thank everyone interviewed in this book—their time and generous quotes not only enriched the text, but they brought additional insight into Alma. This book could not have happened without the efforts and faith placed in it by agent Kay McCauley of the Pimlico Agency, editors Kelly Sinanis, Gail Fortune and copyeditor Christy Wagner, managing editor Erica Rose, and art director Judy Murello. Thanks to Barbara Hall and the Margaret Herrick Library at the Motion Picture Academy of Arts and Sciences.

Special thanks to Universal Pictures for their continuing support.

Laurent Bouzereau would personally like to thank Pat Hitchcock O'Connell and her family, especially Mary, Tere and Katie for giving him the opportunity to work on this book. Special thanks to film historian Kevin Brownlow, and for continuing support, Micheline, Daniel, Cécile and Géraldine Bouzereau, Markus Keith, Colleen A. Benn, Martin Cohen, Michael Stradford, and Sue Williams.

A portion of the proceeds from this book will go to the Cystic Fibrosis Foundation.

INTRODUCTION:
THE WOMAN BEHIND THE MAN

*"The Hitchcock touch had four hands and two were
Alma's."*

—CHARLES CHAMPLIN, FILM CRITIC / HISTORIAN

*L*ONG BEFORE THE recent movement to recognize
women in film, a petite but vibrant sixteen-year-old girl
with long, dark curls from Nottingham, England, launched her
film career in the editing room at Twickenham Studios—some
time in advance of her future husband, I might add. This book
is a tribute to my mother, Alma Reville Hitchcock, the consummate mother, wife, and woman behind the renowned
director, my father, Alfred Hitchcock.

Growing up, my life was permeated by film, so it should come as no surprise that my parents even met in a cinematic way; a bit of mystery and suspense, some romance, and of course, humor to top it all off. How my parents creatively and emotionally collaborated is an almost legendary tale. When my mother did not like a script, my father would immediately abandon the idea. Although he would generally dismiss a bad review, he always paid careful attention to what his wife had to say about his pictures. She maintained her creative involvement in his films and in his career to the end. She advised him on script material, casting, and all aspects of the production. Frequently, she co-wrote the screenplays and stood discreetly at his side during production, in the editing room, and at the launching of each picture. She would usually be present on the set on the first and last days of shooting and occasionally in between, but it was in the evening that my parents discussed the current film. Was the script working? Were the actors behaving? It is notoriously known that Hitch, as my mother and his close friends called him, was bored during filming because he had already done so much preparation that it was just a matter of getting the shots on film. Pre-production on my father's films was most crucial simply because that was when he made all the important decisions with Alma as his closest collaborator.

My mother's contributions were enormous and of course well known to our family, friends and my parents' creative colleagues. But this really became public record in 1978, when my father received the Life Achievement Award from the American Film Institute. In his acceptance speech, he named my mother as having given him:

"the most affection, appreciation, encouragement, and constant collaboration."

∼〇

MY MOTHER CERTAINLY was not the typical Hollywood mother and wife I saw in friends' homes. My life at home with my parents was, quite naturally to me, *normal*. It's true, our house was often filled with luminaries of the silver screen and our meals were delightful rituals of Alma's cooking replete with flown-in delicacies from abroad, but Alma (I called her Mama) cooked them herself, and Hitch (I called him Daddy) helped clean up. I thought this was a delightful and unusual departure from most Hollywood homes, therefore, it must be very like every other child's home growing up in the 1930s, '40s, and '50s. Our home was modest. Our lifestyle, simple. For me, the ease in which my mother monitored the house and worked in twinned association with my father was perfect and natural.

When I matured and became a mother myself, I realized Alma had many lives: She had her role as a wife and collaborator to Daddy, as mother to me, grandmother to my children, and great-grandmother, too (Alma and Hitch both knew their first great-grandchild, Melissa). Mama made remarkable contributions of creativity and devotion in everything and everyone she touched. But she steadfastly tried to not attract attention to herself. She did not need nor want to be in the glaring public eye. It would have distracted her too much from her family life, which became paramount after I was born. She accomplished the work she loved without having to deal with the rules and pretense of the so-called Hollywood life. Hitch, on the other hand, was a born celebrity. That, coupled with the inestimable donation of his work over the years, has provided much fodder for writers and critics. I imagine both Hitch and Alma would have been disappointed by some of what's been written, although ultimately, like myself, they would not have cared that much. They looked at life with a sense of humor, and I have happily inherited that from them.

After participating in many documentaries on the Hitchcock legacy, I felt it was time for me to revisit and honor the past. But rather than approach the story of my family through the famous role of my father, it was important to me to reveal the woman behind the man and illustrate this portrait with private family photos and with personal stories about Alma and Hitch and their life together.

Our memories are so rich with Mama's warmth and guidance, yet so little has actually been written about her inspirational involvement in my father's contribution to film history. Alma's name is present on the credits of several of the Hitchcock's best titles: *The Lodger* (1927) (Adaptation by Alma Reville), *The 39 Steps* (1935) (Continuity: Alma Reville), *Suspicion* (1941) (Screenplay by Samson Raphaelson, Joan Harrison, Alma Reville), *Shadow of a Doubt* (1943) (Screenplay by Thornton Wilder, Sally Benson, and Alma Reville), to name a few. But it was always obvious to me that even if her name didn't necessarily appear on the films, Alma's participation was constant. As I researched this book, I found not only confirmation of Alma's creative participation, but my newly awakened understanding and appreciation that her role went beyond what I already knew. In reading her notes on certain screenplays, in talking to some of my father's collaborators, and in remembering some of her remarks while watching the first cut of a film, I became fascinated with how deeply instrumental my mother was.

While this book pays homage to Alma, it is also an opportunity to focus on the influence she had on the way women were perceived and brought to life in my father's films. Women characters played a remarkable role in Hitchcock's films, and in his own familial life Hitch was surrounded by women: Mama and me, and later on, his three granddaughters and, as I said, one of his great-granddaughters, Melissa. Today I have a total of seven grandchildren: six girls and one boy. I definitely would like to add here that I do not recognize any of my family in Daddy's films—as he always used to say: "It's only a *mooovie!*"

At work, Daddy also surrounded himself with women: Joan Harrison, collaborator on many of the scripts and producer of the television show *Alfred Hitchcock Presents*; his personal assistant, Peggy Robertson; his secretary, Carol Stevens; and his costume designer, Edith Head. Most memorable of course, to audiences at least, are the actresses he worked with on more than one occasion: Ingrid Bergman, Grace Kelly, Joan Fontaine, and Tippi Hedren, to name just a few.

⌁

MAMA'S STORY BEGINS at the turn of the century in England, where she was born. In these pages, we discover her childhood and her early years as an actress, as well as her humble beginnings behind the scenes. Her encounter with Daddy follows. Then come the evolution of their collaboration on the first films, their marriage, the birth of their only child—myself— and the great film classics they made in England.

We moved to America in 1939. There, and with the help of Alma, Hitch would increasingly make an amazing impact on the art of filmmaking; his craft and vision revolutionized the film industry worldwide. Yet with Alma (and myself) at his side, he remained simple and very much a family man.

To make this intimate portrait of Alma complete, we take trips around the world, we reveal how food played a huge role in Daddy's films but was just as important at home, and we visit the different homes we lived in throughout our years in England and in Hollywood, learning that both my parents were also great art collectors. Thanks to this book, I was also able for the first time to reminisce about my acting debut on the New York stage and about my adventures with Alma during some very exciting times.

Interlaced with this portrait of Alma is information about the great Hitchcock film classics—snippets of dialogue, behind-the-scenes stories, and more. We've spoken about Mama with celebrities, close friends and members of the family, validating her influence as a filmmaker and as a loving wife, mother, and grandmother. As I said, Mama was a great cook—she was famous for it. She collected recipes and made up her own menus, many of which I've provided in this book.

I BEGAN THINKING about writing a book about Alma in 1998. The centennial of my parents' birth was still a year away, but already I was receiving constant phone calls from people all over the world planning television documentaries, articles, and books on my father's life and career. But what about my mother, I thought? She is always acknowledged somewhere, somehow—but never is she singled out as an artist in her own right. I decided it was my duty to make sure she was appropriately remembered once and for all.

Starting this book, I felt a bit at a disadvantage. How much does one really know about one's own parents' childhood and their early life? Quickly, I realized there was a lot I didn't know. I suppose the obvious reason was that we moved to America when I was still very young, and then there was a primary motivation in our small family to never look back but only ahead. Back then, one didn't travel back and forth easily across the Atlantic—so quite naturally, after Hitch and Alma moved to America, they lost touch with many of their friends. To prepare for this book, I looked at many photographs, family albums, and home movies (even away from movie studios, the camera never stopped rolling at home). Whether it was documented by my father or my mother, every step of my young life was captured either on film or in a photograph. My father was always clowning around, trying to make me laugh or elicit a response to capture—and he most often succeeded. Alma and Hitch both looked so comfortable and happy in their parental roles. I love watching one particularly funny home movie of my second birthday, where my parents had given me a toy kitchen set as a gift and I served cake

around to them, several friends, and family. I was eternally their child but also often, as the only one, a joyful and trusted companion. I was immediately treated like an adult, so it seemed natural to let me take charge of my own birthday party.

A prevailing trait I knew about Alma—and my own daughters confirm it when we speak of her—is that she rarely ever talked about her childhood or even about herself. Some might say that was because she was shy, but she just wasn't the type of person to reminisce. She and my father lived very much in the moment. On the other hand, as much as she didn't care about discussing her life, she loved to look at her old photo albums and watch our old home movies over and over. And I suspect that perhaps she would have loved the opportunity of revisiting her past, as is so common today. Had she written this book, I think she might have been surprised to realize how much she had accomplished. I know she would have been surprised at how much people would have been fascinated by her own story.

As the book progressed, I grew fascinated to learn about Alma's ancestors and about her early days in Nottingham where she was born. It turned out that my search for my mother's roots vaguely began like a Hitchcock mystery:

In late March of 1998, I put an ad in the local Nottingham newspaper (*The Evening Post*), asking anyone who knew anything about Mama and her family to contact me. Lawrence Geary, a local film enthusiast, got in touch with me and revealed that Alma's Nottingham origins had already been acknowledged. Indeed, in July 1996, Nottingham's Lord Mayor unveiled several plaques to mark sites connected with 100 years of cinema in the city. Each plaque was placed strategically throughout the city. One plaque was placed near where my mother was born and was dedicated to Alma Lucy Reville. The plaque read: "Alma Lucy Reville, Screenwriter—Film Editor, wife of Sir Alfred Hitchcock, born at 69 Caroline Street, St. Anns, 14 August 1899." Unfortunately, the plaque was stolen! Lawrence Geary then decided to beat the odds. When a local theater called The Broadway was revamped, he had a small plaque put on one of the seats that read: "Alma Lucy Reville, born in St. Ann's—Mrs. Alfred Hitchcock." Whoever stole the plaque was never found. An unsatisfactory ending to a mystery, but a lucky turn of events for me. I had tangible proof that people remembered my mother—and that there was genuine interest in her as a film personality. I eventually had another plaque installed at Nottingham's St. Ann's Library.

Alma would never have wanted to write about her life and her career; she was too modest to even think about it, or to think it important. On one occasion, someone approached her to be featured in a book on female screenwriters; the offer was politely declined. However, I think she would be happy with this book because it is written from the heart—a heart she and Daddy encouraged me to share with people. I write this with enduring respect and admiration—just the way I was taught to

meet life and the people in my path. It is, after all, a love letter to my parents, Alma and Hitch.

Pat Hitchcock O'Connell

I FIRST MET Pat Hitchcock when I was doing a documentary on the making of *Psycho.* I was immediately taken by her charm, humor, and incredible knowledge of film. To me, Pat was already more than Alfred Hitchcock's daughter; she was an actress and, I'll admit being occasionally somewhat starstruck, I could not get over the fact that I was in the presence of some-one whose work I admired in addition to her lineage. I first saw Pat in *Psycho,* in which she had a small but memorable scene in the real estate office, opposite Janet Leigh. I then saw her in *Strangers on a Train* and *Stage Fright,* in which she showed her sense of humor and proved she could steal the fire from any other star. Like her mother, Alma, Pat was also making her con-tribution to the Hitchcock legacy. After marriage, Pat became a

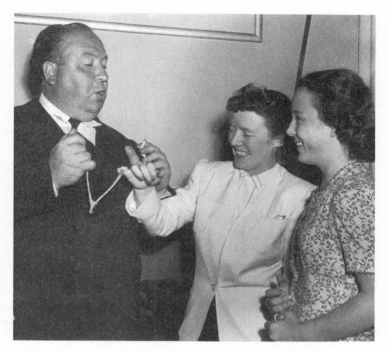

mother and, later on, a grandmother, all the while a devoted daughter to Alma and Hitch. She was there for them then in the same devoted and understated family manner she experienced. With this book, she still is.

Through the years, I made many other Hitchcock documentaries with Pat, and at some point, she indicated she was writing a book about her mother. I knew from my many conversations with Pat that Alma had been a great collaborator on her husband's, Alfred Hitchcock's, films. I immediately thought the book was an amazing idea. Furthermore, I thought it was an important idea, and I was thrilled and honored when Pat asked me to help her with it. The generosity of Pat's entire family—her three amazing daughters, their inspiring children, and their encouraging husbands—made this experience a dream come true. I never thought I knew everything about the Hitchcock legacy, but after spending time with Pat and her family, I realized, how much more there was to learn. Pat wanted this book to be inspiring; Alma was, after all, a pioneer in her field for two reasons: Film barely existed when she was born, and very few women creatively worked in that industry. Pat also wanted this book to be more than a film book. It's about family, food, and travel and still satisfies the film buff in all of us. It's really the portrait of an era. In researching the book, Pat and I scrutinized the family's home movies, looked at countless pictures, and watched the films over and over. While Pat and her daughters reminisced, we pieced together memories and happily realized we were telling a story that was long overdue. And as far as I'm concerned, with *Alma*, the Hitchcock touch might have had four hands, but with Pat, it had six.

Laurent Bouzereau

YOUNG AND INNOCENT

MY MOTHER CLAIMED that she was always exposed to the world of movies. How could she avoid the inevitable? She and her family lived right around the corner from Twickenham Studios, where her father had a job in the costume department. The first film to come out of Twickenham was *The House of Temperley* (based on the novel *Rodney Stone* by Sir Arthur Conan Doyle), in 1913, produced by an American, Harold Shaw, for the newly formed London Film Company. Twickenham, formerly a skating rink, was the largest film studio in the United Kingdom at that time. The London Film Company had been created by Dr. R. T. Jupp, the managing director of one of the largest exhibition circuits, Provincial Cinematograph Theaters, Ltd. Jupp was one of the first to build actual movie theaters in England. Usually, people of my parents' generation would see films at converted shops.

My grandmother, Lucy, took her daughter to movies very early on, and quickly Alma acquired a passion for film. But apparently there was some objection from relatives to Lucy taking Alma to the movies: "Oh, you shouldn't take Alma there. She'll only pick up fleas," they would say. Thank God Lucy didn't let that stop her.

When Alma was a teenager, most of the top box-office stars were Americans. British production companies were a bit slow to embrace the potential commercial appeal of actors. Also, the biggest studios of the time did not use close-ups, and performers were always seen in master shots. Eventually, British stars of the stage and music hall began appearing in films, and audiences started recognizing certain names and faces. By 1910, the public—which included Alma and Hitch—was eager to follow the off-screen lives of their favorite actors. Violet Hopson (a name only my parents and film historians would probably recognize) was the first British actress to receive the same treatment as her American counterparts and was groomed for stardom by a film studio. When my mother started in the film business a few years later, other stars such as Ivor Novello and Betty Balfour were getting established.

Alma loved bicycling to visit her father at Twickenham Studios. Watching the actors at work fascinated her. When she left school at the tender age of sixteen, her career actually began with her working away from soundstages; her film education developed in the cutting room instead. As I have said, my mother was very modest; she never spoke much about her humble beginnings in the business, despite the fact that she was not only talented and had mastered her craft but was also very well respected. I think she was definitely a pioneer.

Years later, when we were living in Hollywood, I bought a small Super 8 Moviola to splice together some of our family's home movies. To this day, I remember her look of interest as she watched me with the machine. As her eyes lit up, I could tell it evoked some memory in her, and she became nostalgic.

∼

AUGUST 14, 1899, was a fine, dry summer day in England. Though there were some showers in the west and southwest of England, the weather was just lovely 120 miles north of London where my mother was born in Nottingham, only a few hours after my father's birth on August 13th in Leytonstone. Many talents who my parents would eventually work with were born in 1899, including Noel Coward, Charles Laughton (who would work with my parents and star in *Jamaica Inn* [1939] and *The Paradine Case* [1947]), George Cukor, Irving Thalberg, James Cagney, and Charles Bennett (who would write the scripts for several of my parents' early pictures).

My maternal grandfather, Matthew Edward Reville, was a lace warehouseman (Nottingham was primarily a city of lace). He began working as an apprentice in 1881, and after holding several other jobs, he became a traveling salesman in 1926. He was one of three children of George Edward Reville, an ironsmith, and Jane Bailey Reville, a hosiery worker, who also came from a working-class family. (Her father, Thomas Bailey, was a nailmaker.)

My grandmother, Lucy Owen, three years younger than her husband, worked as a "lace hand." She was born on November 3, 1866. Her proud parents were Hugh and Ann Dance Owen, and she had two sisters, Clara and Alma (whom my mother was named after). Hugh was a retired military man (my grandparents' marriage certificate lists Lucy's father's profession as "Gentleman") who died in April of 1891, five months before his daughter's wedding.

Mama's parents were married at the Castle Gate Independent Chapel, at 74 Union Road in Nottingham on August 25, 1891; Matthew was 27, Lucy, 24. A man named George Archer Price

Aunt Eveline, my grandparents Lucy and Matthew, and Mama.

and Annie Elizabeth Reville (Matthew's younger sister—he had another sister named Nellie) were witnesses at the ceremony. My grandparents' first child was a beautiful daughter named Eveline and, on August 14, 1899, Mama was born in the home of her parents, at 69 Caroline Street, Nottingham.

Shortly after Alma was born, the family moved to Twickenham, west of London. As a child, Alma had lovely long curls, prompting an unfortunate incident at the funeral of King

Edward VII in 1910, creating a fear and apprehension that followed her whole life. King Edward was the eldest son of Queen Victoria and Prince Albert. Born in 1841 in Buckingham Palace, he became Prince of Wales when he was two months old and King of Great Britain and Ireland and Emperor of India in 1901. The King was 69 when he passed away, and Mama was eleven years old when she accompanied her father to watch his funeral cortege. My grandfather had put Mama up on his shoulders to watch the procession go by, and as he set her down, her hair got caught in a man's coat button and she suddenly got dragged down as the stranger walked on. At eleven years old, Alma was quite small, and although she grew a little, like her own mother, she remained petite. I know Mama didn't like crowds. I often wondered if the incident at the king's funeral and the fact that she only stood at four feet eleven were the reasons why she feared she could easily disappear in large gatherings.

My mother did not have many friends growing up—Hitch had a rather similar solitary childhood. However, Alma was very close to her family, especially her mother and sister. Alma had strong family values and ties. She did everything she could for her family. After World War II started, Alma immediately went to London and brought both her mother and sister back to America with her. My grandfather, whom I never knew, had already died at the age of sixty-four, a year after my parents were married. My memory of my grandmother was that she was shy, petite, and resembled my mother. She lived modestly, and she never spoiled me; you didn't spoil children in those days.

Aunt Eveline, on the other hand, was very different from Mama in a number of ways. Taller and heavier than Alma, she had unusual features; I recall her thin lips. At some point, her name in the family became Eva. She became Bingo to me after her arrival in America. I have no idea where it came from, but it stayed. Until the day she died, we called her Bingo! In 1939, when my mother transported her mother and sister to

Aunt Eveline—who I called Bingo—and Mama in their teens.

America, my parents found a place for them in Westwood, California, and I stayed with them quite often. They lived in a small apartment on Ashton Avenue, down the street from a movie theater. I remember many nights when the three of us went to the movies together. It was a simple pleasure but always great fun and memorable to me.

Bingo married at the age of fifty-three. By then, she had moved on her own and worked at the Beverly Wilshire Hotel in the accounting department, where she met a British widower named Albert. Albert was a waiter, and after their marriage, they moved to a small house off Olympic Boulevard.

Alma and Bingo mostly got along well but occasionally my mother was a little testy with her sister. Alma was definitely more sophisticated, yet she was very understated in that sophistication; her life with Hitch and their work set their lifestyle apart from the usual. Bingo was simple and less complicated. Did my father get along with her? Not really. In fact, there was a similar gap between my father's own sister and brother; they loved each other but grew apart as the world they lived in changed. We lost Bingo in 1970—she died suddenly at her home early one morning. Albert passed away a few years later.

At an early age, my mother was diagnosed with St. Vitus Dance, also called Syndenham's Chorea, which is a major manifestation of acute rheumatic fever. It commonly occurs between the ages of seven and fourteen, mostly in girls. The disease (its name stems from the Greco-Latin word implying the act of dancing) is characterized by irregular movements and muscular weakness. As a result of the disease, Alma had to stay out of school for a total of two years. Throughout her life, and despite her accomplishments as a self-taught film editor and writer, she remained extremely self-conscious and sensitive about her lack of formal education. In later years, she was thrilled to see my three daughters go off to college; proper education and schooling were essential to my parents and most keenly to my mother who felt she had missed out on it because of her early poor health. Curiously—and luckily, I might add—my mother never became a hypochondriac; in fact, she was quite the opposite. For instance, when I was a child we traveled regularly to Capri and Naples, Italy, and, for some reason, she would always get strep throat. Yet she never worried about it, she just accepted it. My father, on the other hand, especially when he became older, was often concerned over small ailments. You'd say to him, "How are you?" and he'd respond, "Oh, I have a cold."

When I was a child, Alma was never overly protective or even paranoid of diseases, despite her own childhood medical history. At the same time, she was very strict when it came to my education. I was in a private school run by nuns until I was eight years old. Then, my parents sent me to boarding school. I hated it and I was miserable the whole time. In England, and Europe in general, it wasn't unusual to send your children to boarding school at an early age. Still, I resented it. The school was about an hour outside London, and my parents would

come down to visit to take me out to lunch, but I couldn't go home until the end of the term. I slept in a dormitory with about twenty other girls. It was very rigorous. I told my parents how I felt, but there was nothing I could do to persuade them to take me out of school. I felt like I had been put in jail. As bad as it was, I never harbored any resentment toward my parents; they explained to me that it was necessary. I had no choice, and eventually I understood their desire for my classic education. By then, despite the fact that my parents were part of the film industry, they certainly did not abide by the typical Hollywood standards when it came to raising me. I was never spoiled unnecessarily or treated in any special, privileged way because of who they were. A lesson I learned early on was that you don't necessarily get everything you want in life, and my parents made sure I never lost track of reality. Regardless of the way I felt about boarding school, the thing I loved about my parents is that we maintained a constant interesting dialogue. I think that was a bit unusual for the time. In my home, we talked about everything with curiosity and enthusiasm. Interestingly, my parents treated me like an adult. They had complete faith and trust in me. Not being treated like a child meant that at the age of three, my parents began taking me to the theater. I don't remember what I saw, but I do remember my fascination with stage musicals in London from that day forward. In unusual ways, my parents were quite liberal by exposing me to their own taste and culture early on while maintaining a very strong sense of values. I was fortunate to develop a strong sense for what I wanted to do later in life—to act. In that sense, I believe I am very similar to my mother. She always knew what she wanted and simply went for it.

ALMA: THE REWIND GIRL

*B*Y THE TIME Alma began her career, British cinema was still in its infant years. But a few things had already taken place that showed that the film industry was at least developing. The production, exhibition, and distribution of movies were evolving, and rules were being created. The first indoor studio was built in 1899 (the year my mother and father were born); in 1909, the Cinematograph Act passed laws outlining theater safety regulations; and in 1912, the British Board of Censors was established. There were two ratings, U (Universal) and A (adult).

Alma got a job in the editing room as a "rewind girl" for the London Film Company at Twickenham Studios, where my grandfather worked in the studio's costume department. Alma had full-blown "filmitis" and would be the first one to acknowledge that she was "film mad." Her first impulse was that she wanted to be on the sets, perhaps even as an actress, but her father thought she should first see the seamy side of film by starting as an editor. Twickenham was, in fact, the only place for her to find work, having no real experience. Mama started in the film business four years earlier than Daddy. In those days, films were cut and spliced completely by hand. No electricity was used. It was a very precise and tedious job, which probably, and unfortunately, further damaged her eyes; she was farsighted and always had to wear glasses.

This must have been both a very exciting and scary time. The industry was so young, and there was no way of knowing where it would go or how fast it would grow. No one really knew that films would eventually talk, that color would replace black and white, and that it would become the vast worldwide industry and empire it is today. I'm not suggesting that people were making things up as they went, but there was definitely a lot of experimenting, a lot of trial and error going on. On the other hand, for someone like my mother, it was an opportunity to grow alongside an industry that was practically her own age. They had that in common and as two siblings of the same generation; they could learn from one another and continue to evolve together.

In the cutting room, Alma was as happy as a child with a new toy, but she did admit that, although she wasn't daunted with her job, she began to see how interesting a salaried job at a studio was, and how much less precarious than film acting. Alma volunteered for odd jobs, trying to make herself useful to everyone. In the cutting room, she reached a technical proficiency so expert that she was entrusted with the cutting of the actual film negative, which also meant she was making more money.

Alma got closer to the flame, so to speak, and worked as a floor secretary on the sets. Quickly, she graduated to a double position: editor and continuity girl. Again, the job was very precise and required immense attention and a great sense of organization. She was responsible for the order in which the scenes were shot and for the overall consistency of the scenes. That particular job still exists in film, and I'm proud that my mother was a pioneer in that field as well. Alma's duties would progress to that of an assistant director within a few years.

However, films were, of course, put together very differently back then, and the development of *the art* of telling stories on celluloid was still in it's infant years. They would shoot scenes wide, without doing close-ups on the actors. Therefore, no editing was needed, just the splicing of one scene to another. Editing style began to emerge especially in America, Russia and Germany. But at that point, the profession of "editor" really meant gluing the different parts together and was pretty much a technical job. Things eventually took a turn for the better, especially when filmmakers such as my father appeared on the scene and revolutionized the art of telling stories on film, literally inventing a visual language and style—which contemporary filmmakers still try to emulate. The name Hitchcock is used as an adjective today, and there's no doubt that behind it stands the brilliance of my father as well as of my mother.

～

APPARENTLY, THE FIRST film my mother worked on was a costume picture. "When I saw the picture put together," she once wrote in an article, "I saw that I had made so many mistakes with their clothes. Here this girl would come into the hallway with mittens on, would go into the other room and wouldn't have the mittens on, and the other way when she left. It was a wonder I wasn't thrown out!" Alma certainly had a sense of humor, even about her own mistakes. Although I do suspect that back then she must have thought she might lose her job. But again, everyone was learning, and her mistakes probably went unnoticed or were passed off as creative decisions.

By growing with the film industry, her knowledge and background would become invaluable to her future husband, Alfred Hitchcock. While my father deserves to be called—as he has on numerous occasions—the Messiah of British cinema, Alma was, due to her seniority over him in the film industry, one of his most trusted apostles.

One highlight for Mama was working on the production of *Hearts of the World* (1918), directed by the legendary D. W. Griffith. Griffith was already a recognized genius and the industry's true first director/producer. When Alma met him, he had directed many films and at least two classics: *The Birth of a Nation* (1915) and *Intolerance* (1916). *Hearts of the World* starred the famous American silent movie stars Lillian Gish and her sister Dorothy Gish, Erich Von Stroheim, the famous Austrian actor and director (one of his most memorable roles is as the director-turned-butler in *Sunset Boulevard* [1950]), received credit as an actor as well as technical advisor; and Noel Coward, who played in the film as "the boy with wheelbarrow," and would become an international figure in the world of show business, wearing many different hats as writer, composer, and director. How stimulating it must have been to Alma to be part of such an exciting project—and how inspiring for her to be a witness to the production, even in a very modest position. Working in any capacity on a D. W. Griffith picture in those days would be the equivalent of getting any job on a Steven Spielberg movie today. Another important thing to point out is that my mother was in essence being exposed to American filmmakers and receiving an education from people who were far more advanced than their British counterparts. Obviously, those experiences were preparing her for a transition that would take place some twenty-five years later, when we would move to America.

MY MOTHER KEPT several photo albums with behind-the-scenes photographs of films she worked on. Alma worked a lot and was always fascinated with the process. Her photographs are documents of an era. She had a sharp and creative eye; the composition in her photographs are professional and indicate she instinctively knew how to look through a lens. By the age of twenty, Alma had also been in front of the camera—she would do little bits (that would probably qualify as extra work) as well as small parts for leaders in the film industry such as directors Harold Shaw, George L. Tucker (an American filmmaker who directed a version of *The Prisoner of Zenda* in 1915), and Herbert Brenon. The only really memorable role she had was playing the daughter of politician and Prime Minister Lloyd George in *The Life Story of David Lloyd George* (1918), directed by Maurice Elvey, with whom Alma had been working.

After directing on Broadway, Maurice Elvey returned to his native England and made more than 300 films. Elvey also worked in Hollywood and was at some point head of production at Gaumont British. He always referred to *The Life Story of David Lloyd George* as his most important film. "The part of the young girl, Megan Lloyd George, was played by that charming lady Alma Reville who was to become Mrs. Alfred Hitchcock and at that time used to edit my films for me," Elvey wrote in a book on his career. Lloyd George was played by Norman Page, a well-respected stage actor. However, the film was confiscated under mysterious and questionable reasons. Elvey

On the set of God's Prodigal, *one of the earlier movies that Mama worked on.*

believed his film had been destroyed, along with my mother's portrayal of Megan Lloyd George. Elvey died in 1967. In 1994, the Rt. Hon. Viscount Tenby, the grandson of Lloyd George, sent a collection of memorabilia to the Wales National Film and Television Archive. He had no idea of the content of the collection and—miraculously—amongst the memorabilia, a copy of the film was found. Once restored, Alma's role in *The Life Story of David Lloyd George* could finally be seen, some 78 years later! It is indeed a very small role—she has only a couple of scenes—but I must say it was the strangest feeling to watch

Mama as an actress so many years later. The first screening ever of the film was on April 27, 1996, and the world premiere of the film took place, with live music, on May 5 of that same year at the MGM Cinema in Cardiff in connection with 100 years of cinema in Wales.

Alma never mentioned that she had wished to pursue an acting career after her modest beginnings in *Lloyd George,* but I did find a couple posed pictures of her with her list of credits in the back, indicating that perhaps Alma would have become an actress, had the opportunity presented itself:

"Alma Reville, 19 Sandycoombe Road, St. Margarets on Thames, Middlesex. Age: 20, height: 4 ft. 11 in. (without shoes), hair: light brown (curly), eyes: light brown.

Qualifications: Dance, stage, ballroom, row, cycle, billiards. Good wardrobe.

Experience: Small parts for Harold Shaw, George L. Tucker, Herbert Brenon, Maurice Elvey. Played Megan Lloyd George in *The Life Story of David Lloyd George* from the age of 9 to present day. Also has been producer's assistant to Maurice Elvey for two years."

~⌒

MY MOTHER'S PHOTO albums—"Snaps" she called them— were not only a way for her to chronicle her career. She also took many pictures of her friends and family. At times, she also wrote little captions. Looking at them, I also discovered a lot of names and saw a lot of faces I didn't know: Mrs. Whitmam, Auntie Faith, Lizzie, Mrs. Young (and her baby), Connie Rowe, and Uncle Tim. I discovered where the Revilles went on vacation: Richmond, Minehead, Bournemouth. And when Alma was not taking the pictures, she would pose for one in her horseback-riding outfit. Mama was petite, but looking at the pictures, she seems very different from the other women of

711

Alma Reville
19 Sandycoom
St Margarets
Middl

Age. 20.
Height 4ft 11in (wit
Hair light Brow
Eyes   "   "
Qualifications
Dance - Stage -
Row, Cycle. F
Good waidrobe
Experience :-
Small parts f
George. L. Tucke
Maurice Elve
Played " Imoge
in Ideal's "Life of Lloyd Geor
from the age of 9 to present day
also been producer's assestant
to Maurice Elvey for 2 years

her generation. You see the determination in her eyes, her sense of humor in her smile, and her confidence in her poise. She was a proud and confident young lady. It's no wonder a young man named Alfred Hitchcock fell in love with her at first sight.

ALMA MEETS HITCH

$\mathcal{I}$N 1921, ALMA got a job at Famous Players-Lasky British Producers Ltd., Islington Studios. Adolph Zukor, a Hungarian-born film pioneer who had moved to America, founded Famous Players in 1912. Zukor then merged with an American producer named Jesse L. Lasky, to found Famous Players-Lasky, later to become Paramount. Alma's first assignment in the cutting room was Donald Crisp's *Appearances*. Crisp was a Scottish-born actor who had worked with D. W. Griffith. At the time Alma met him, he was also directing. It was then that she became aware of a harried young man by the name of Alfred Hitchcock. This intriguing young man was rather shy and, although he also had noticed Alma, he took his time before approaching her. I was still in my teens when I once asked

Mama: "How did you and Daddy meet?" She proceeded to tell me the story as if it had just happened, as if she had waited for me to ask the question.

It was in 1921, and Hitch was a newcomer to the film studio where she worked. This was in the days of silent pictures, when dialogue had to be written out on cards (known as subtitles or as spoken titles and later as inter-titles, to differentiate from subtitles on foreign films) and then photographed. So when a young man walked into the studio with an enormous flat package under one arm, Alma immediately understood that the parcel contained inter-titles for *Appearances,* and that this was the new artist who had been hired to design them. Alma confessed she always enjoyed watching a person's first reaction to the confusion of the studio. In those days visitors invariably stopped, spellbound, at the door, gazing in bewilderment at the lights, the cameras, the actors in their makeup, the shouting, and the running. But to my mother, the studio was like home. She was working there and knew everything there was to know about it. People meeting her for the first time would have immediately noticed her confidence and her knowledge. Without ever being conscious of it, she must have been a bit intimidating.

But on the day Alma first saw Hitch, he simply strolled across the set, without paying any attention to anything or anyone around him, and disappeared with his cards into the production office.

Alma was even more perplexed as the weeks passed. She had by then worked at the studio for more than five years and was used to a certain amount of respect and admiration by the newcomers. But this young man, my father, never even noticed her. Hitch and Alma worked at the same studio for two years, and to my mother's knowledge, in all that time he never so much as glanced in her direction. During that time, Alma would edit films such as *Beside the Bonnie Brier Bush* by Donald Crisp in 1921, and *The Man from Home* by George Fitzmaurice in 1922, for which Hitch would design the inter-titles. Looking through Alma's photo albums, it appears she also worked on *God's Prodigal* in 1923, directed by Bart Wynne and Edward Jose and *Tell Your Children* by Donald Crisp.

And then the studio closed down. For months Alma was out of work. She was very upset and scared, but she never showed it. One day the telephone rang. "Miss Reville?" inquired a formal male voice. "This is Alfred Hitchcock. I am assistant director for a new film," the voice went on stiffly. "I wonder if you would accept a position as a cutter on the picture."

∼

MY FATHER, ALFRED Joseph Hitchcock, was born on August 13, 1899, in Leytonstone, England, to William Hitchcock and Emma Jane Whelan. Hitch was the third and last child of the family: His brother, William Jr., was born in 1890, and his sister, Eileen (Nellie), in 1892. Hitch's father had a grocery store and also worked the market at Covent Garden, where my father would shoot his film *Frenzy* in 1972. Hitch was born and raised a Catholic. As a child, my father was curious about everything, but was also very quiet, reserved, and somewhat of a loner. The most significant incident in Hitch's childhood took place when he was five years old. He had apparently done something bad, and his father took him to the local jail and had him locked behind bars for a few minutes. He was then informed this was what happened to naughty boys, hence, my father's notorious phobia of policemen.

Growing up, Hitch attended several different schools, including a boarding school called St. Ignatius College in Stamford Hill, where he received a rather strict Jesuit education. Many years later, my father would acknowledge that he learned fear from his years in Catholic school.

Hitch's parents had been avid theatergoers, and Hitch discovered movies and started going to many movies and reading film magazines in his mid-teens. He liked drawing and decided to take art classes at the London University; his teacher was a well-respected book illustrator named E. J. Sullivan. Realizing his creative talent, Hitch published a short story in June 1919, in *The Henley* (The W. T. Henley Telegraph Company's social club magazine). The story was titled "Gas," and it told the mad adventures of a woman in Paris until we realize she is, in fact, at the dentist, getting a tooth pulled, and under the effects of "gas." That same year, an American film company, Famous Players-Lasky, bought an electrical plant in Islington and created a studio. Hitch was hired to do drawings and sketches and began doing inter-titles. Eventually, Hitch moved his way up to assistant director. And that's when he met Alma Reville.

Hitch's first impression of his future wife was that she was a bit snooty. As mentioned, they worked at the same studio for two years and Hitch never acknowledged Alma. Apparently, the interview was brief, for Alma politely informed her future husband that the salary he offered was inadequate. Alma said "Good afternoon" very sweetly and was halfway down the passage when she heard Hitch calling after her. The discussion was reopened and an amicable arrangement was reached. Mama had a simple explanation for Daddy's behavior toward her: It was unthinkable for a British man to admit that a woman had a better position, and Hitch waited to speak to her until he had a better job than she did, until he was in a position of power. But a connection had been made. From that day on, Alma and Hitch were on their way to a long, sentimental and professional journey.

My father knew how to come up with clever plots for his films. His plots worked just as well in real life; by hiring Alma on a film titled *Woman to Woman* (in 1923), he knew they would spend a lot of time together . . . and so they did.

Woman to Woman was a romance story produced by Michael Balcon, Victor Saville, and John Freedman and directed by Graham Cutts. By then, Hitch had directed a "two-reeler" called

Number Thirteen in 1922, but the film was never completed. Hitch had also directed portions of a remake called *Always Tell Your Wife* (1923—the original film was released in 1914) when the director, Hugh Croise, "fell ill." The picture was completed by both Hitch and Seymour Hicks (who also produced, co-wrote the adaptation of his own play, and starred in the film). *Woman to Woman* was based on a successful play by Michael Morton; Michael Balcon, a giant film figure, founder of Gainsborough Pictures in 1924, and four years later a leader of Gaumont-British Pictures, would play a key role in my father's career. Balcon first hired Hitch as assistant director, but soon Daddy found himself working on the script and on the art direction. (Hitch would receive credit as assistant director, co-screenwriter, and set designer; Alma's credit on the film was editor and she was also in charge of continuity on the set.) The story began during World War I; a British army officer meets a French dancer in Paris, is wounded on the battlefield, and loses his memory. After the war, he returns to England and gets married. Later, the other woman shows up with a child. The story ends tragically with the death of the French girl. Alma and Hitch worked on the production in the summer of 1923 at Islington Studios. Interestingly, the film starred a Hollywood actress, Betty Compson, and thanks to her name alone, *Woman to Woman* was not only well reviewed, but it also became a commercial success. The experience for Alma was amazing and a real breakthrough—although she was apparently not particularly fond of director Graham Cutts. She did not think he was pleasant or professional; he knew very little and Alma felt she and Hitch were doing all the work. Inevitably, the next few productions that followed *Woman to Woman* (*The White Shadow* in 1923 and *The Passionate Adventure* in 1924) were not as successful.

Following a new partnership with German producer Erich Pommer (who at that point had produced Fritz Lang's *The Cabinet of Dr. Caligary* in 1919 and *Doctor Mabuse* in 1922), Hitch and Alma were sent to Neubabelsberg, Germany, to work with Graham Cutts on *The Blackguard* (filmed in 1924 and released in 1925) at the UFA film studios. Again, my father filled many roles on the film and was credited as screenwriter, assistant director, and set designer. Hitch and Alma were even left on their own when Graham Cutts decided to take off with his new girlfriend. Hitch embraced the opportunity he had to observe German filmmakers at work and always acknowledged the influence that the cinema of Fritz Lang, F. W. Murnau, Emil Jannings, and others (including Russian directors) had on his own development as a director.

Because *The Blackguard* was to be made in Germany, both Hitch and Alma had to learn the language. My parents became fluent, and I recall that if they didn't want me to understand what they were saying, they'd speak in German.

An interesting side story about my father and the German language: Daddy's lead-ins for his television series *Alfred Hitchcock Presents* in the sixties had to be translated into other languages. When it came to the German titles, the producers assumed he could read them because they knew he spoke the language. So they just wrote them hoping he would be able to read them. They were surprised when he told them he could not read them at all—he had learned German by ear, phonetically, on his trips there but simply could not write or read it—and neither could Alma!

However, one thing was certain; Daddy did not need to learn any other language but the universal speech of love to ask Mama if she would accept him as husband. But as to be expected, there is a strange twist to that story, too.

HITCH PROPOSES AND COMPLETES
HIS FIRST FILM

ONCE *The Blackguard* was completed, Hitch decided it was time to propose to Alma. But he made sure she could not say no. They were headed back to England on a tiny ship. It was Christmas Eve and a bitter cold stormy night. The waves were enormous and the sea was quite choppy. Alma got seasick and was lying on the bunk of her little cabin, not caring whether she lived or died. She was simply miserable. There was a knock on the door and an unusually disheveled Hitch appeared, his hair wildly blown about, his coat drenched, and his face bland as ever. It was at that opportune moment that my father proposed: "Would you marry me?" he asked. Alma was too sick to lift her head from the pillow. She groaned, nodded her head, and burped. I guess a woman is never so ill that she doesn't know an answer to *that* question!

This experience would leave an everlasting impression on my father, and marriage proposals would often be featured in his films. Possibly the most famous one of all takes place on top on Mount Rushmore in *North by Northwest* (1959). Cary Grant and Eva Marie Saint are trying to escape from the bad guys, and in the middle of it all, Cary says, "If we ever get out of this alive, let's go back to New York on the train together, all right?" "Is that a proposition," she asks. And he replies, "It's a proposal, sweetie." Nothing as dramatic happened to my parents, but I guess the outcome was just as successful in real life as it would be in the movies.

Back home, Graham Cutts was set to direct another film titled *The Prude's Fall*. The experience was very challenging for both Hitch and Alma. In short, Cutts realized that my father was overshadowing him and requested he not be hired on his next picture (*The Rat*, starring Ivor Novello). This turned out to be a blessing in disguise. One evening, Hitch proudly announced to Alma that Michael Balcon had offered him to direct a film titled *The Pleasure Garden*. There was, of course, a job for Alma as well. Her credit would be assistant director and continuity.

My parents were not married yet, but, as my father would have put it, they weren't living in sin either; they were still very pure. At that point, Alma was still living with her parents in Twickenham, and Daddy with his mother in Leyonstone. My mother told me how they would have supper at the end of a day's work and how they would go to the movies together.

Meanwhile, Alma was starting to get attention from the press. In fact, she was mentioned in a short article by P. L. Mannock on October 8, 1925, in *Kinematograph Weekly* magazine, showing how well respected and how established her name was in the industry. The article explained how Alma, a clever and experienced little lady, was "a striking example of those important assistant filmmakers upon whom the limelight of publicity seldom, if ever, blazes." The article concluded, "She had much to do with the finish of all of Graham Cutts' big pictures, and Gainsborough is to be congratulated on the retention of her exclusive services, the value of which everyone who knows her will confirm." Accompanying those flattering words was a pretty picture of Alma smiling under a fashionable hat. My parents' collaboration and career were evolving, as was their romance—and both would be put to test on *The Pleasure Garden*.

The Pleasure Garden was a rather complex drama about two chorus girls at the Pleasure Garden Theatre, Patsy (Virginia Valli) and Jill (Carmelita Geraghty), and two men stationed in the colonies, Levet (Miles Mander) and his colleague Hugh (John Stuart). Simply told, Patsy marries Levet, and after their honeymoon on Lake Como, Levet leaves for the colonies. Although Jill is engaged to Hugh, she isn't devoted to him—she later marries a prince. When Patsy comes to join Levet, she finds him in the arms of a native woman. Levet stages the drowning of his mistress, making it look like suicide. As he is about to murder Patsy, he is shot by another English expatriate. There is hope for Patsy, as Hugh who, having been abandoned by Jill, is ready to embark on a new romance. The screenplay was by Eliot Stannard, who would collaborate with my father on a total of eight movies. The script was based on a novel by Oliver Sandys.

The production of my father's official first feature film was rather tumultuous. For one thing there never was enough money, and, at one point, there was simply no money! My parents went to Germany for pre-production work (the film was to be shot on location in Italy and at the Emelka Studios in Munich). Hitch was set to go to Italy with a small crew, while Alma was to go to Cherbourg, France, to pick up the two American actresses: Virginia Valli (one of Universal's biggest stars) and Carmelita Geraghty. After Cherbourg, Alma was to take them to Paris to buy their wardrobe for the film and would then be on their way to Italy to meet my father. When the two women got off *The Aquitania,* they were carrying tons of luggage but they still had to get the wardrobe for the film. Alma bought what was needed in Paris, but it ended up costing a lot more than she had initially anticipated. Then, to make matters worse, the two actresses insisted on staying at Claridges Hotel, but Alma had only budgeted for The Westminster, a modest hotel on the Rue de la Paix. When Alma finally arrived in Italy to meet Hitch with the two actresses, she was practically penniless. My father was upset. For one thing, Carmelita Geraghty was not needed in the scenes that were to be shot in that particular location, and now they had to pay for her hotel room. The thing that Mama did not know was that Hitch had had his share of money trouble as well; everything had gone wrong for him, too, and Hitch had been counting on Alma to save him from having to beg the production to wire him some more cash. No such luck. Hitch and Alma were in trouble, not to mention the fact that Hitch did not want Ms. Valli to find out this was his first film. Thank God for Mama—she was there to calm him down when he went into a panic about the situation and to keep up appearances. And at one point, Hitch sent Alma to ask Ms. Valli for money. Alma, charming and, let's face it, desperate, managed to get the cash. During filming, Hitch was very nervous working with his American actress, and after each shot, he would discreetly turn to Alma and ask: "Was that all right?" My mother would remain the only one to ever see that side of Daddy. He was usually calm and composed under every other circumstance.

After location shooting was completed, Hitch was worried that the Hollywood actress and her friend were going to request an expensive meal on the train back to Germany. So again, he sent Alma to ask them. Luckily, they didn't care for "train" food and had brought their own snack. That meant Alma and Hitch had enough money for a meal! Was that a light at the end of the tunnel? Not quite. The train was delayed, they missed their connection, and they had to stay in a hotel. The next day, Hitch made one last false move and accidentally broke a window on the train while loading the luggage and was fined for it. My parents barely made it back to Munich. Needless to say, they were thrilled to be finishing the film in the safety of the studio. Come to think of it, my father always loathed going on location for any film, and I wouldn't be surprised if that experience might have had something (or a lot) to do with it. Following the end of filming, my parents had their first—and rare—disagreement. It had to do with the editing of the picture, which my mother supervised; my father said it was "flashy"! What I believe he meant was that the scenes were more edited than usual. With her editing skills, Alma had made the film more dynamic but might have overdone it a bit. Interestingly enough, after seeing the film, Michael Balcon thought it looked very American. (I'm not sure if he meant that as a compliment or not.) For instance, there was a scene in which Levet was shot that shocked one of the German producers, who felt it was too brutal to be shown! In fact, the original title was changed in Germany to something less provocative: *The Maze of Passion*. In the end, the film was well received. *The London Daily Express* even referred to Daddy as a "young man with a master mind," and in Germany, one critic pointed at my father's clever use of humor in some of the film's most dramatic scenes (a trademark Daddy would perfect in the films and years to come). *The Pleasure Garden* had been a real test on both Hitch and Alma—the result was quite extraordinary and confirmed their compatibility as full-time partners.

Alma had watched Hitch quite closely during the most challenging aspects of the production; even under pressure, Hitch tried to remain calm. Through the years, Alma observed that Hitch was at his calmest on a film set. She would tell me she never once saw his face lose what she referred to as his "mystic calm." She had worked on other films she described as "little town riots," where the script was changed at the last minute, the props were missing, an extra tripped over the lighting cables, the makeup man was late—and all this with the director screaming on top of his lungs. But when she watched Hitch shooting a picture, she immediately noticed order and precision around him. His sets were always quiet, too. Early on, Alma was intrigued by Hitch's ability to walk on to a set with such confidence. That's when she realized that it all had to do with preparation—it was a matter of planning ahead.

Emergencies did arise, of course, in spite of Daddy's advance planning, and they were always met with the same calm. Mama once told me about a terrible day when a gigantic film crane rolled over Hitch's foot. Six men were seated on it, and not one of them realized what had happened until Hitch murmured courteously, "Could you possibly remove your crane? Currently it is resting on my foot."

~~~

THANKS TO *THE Pleasure Garden,* Hitch would get noticed although the film was not yet released. And Alma was also receiving her share of attention. Her position in the film industry (especially for such a young woman) continued to attract notice from the press. I was pleasantly surprised when I found another old newspaper article dated December 1925, published in a British film magazine called *The Picturegoer,* showing that Alma was publicly respected and acknowledged as a pioneer in her own right. She occupied a unique position in European films. The article was titled "Alma in Wonderland: An interesting article, proving that a woman's place is not always at home." "Little Alma Reville is nothing like as unsophisticated as she looks, as some tough film guys have discovered to their cost," the article said. She is described as always smiling, and as being calm, efficient, and able to assume successfully "those heavy responsibilities which fall upon those grouped around the director." According to the article, there were two secrets about Alma. One was that she had a pair of horn-rimmed glasses she never wore. The second was that she had never had the time to get married. The second, at least, was about to change.

THE FIRST "HITCHCOCK" MOVIE
AND A MARRIAGE

$\mathcal{M}$Y FATHER'S NEXT film, *The Mountain Eagle* (1925/released 1927), was, in his own words, "a very bad movie." With Alma as assistant director, the film starred an American actress, Nita Naldi. Hitch and Alma had met Naldi while making *The Pleasure Garden* when she was the last-minute replacement to the native woman murdered by Miles Mander in the film. Naldi was very proud of her long fingernails, which Daddy thought looked ridiculous. He had to convince her to shed them during filming. Naldi did end up being quite charming and funny (she had a very strong Brooklyn accent). She traveled with an older gentleman with white hair. My parents would get together with them in Paris while they were on their honeymoon. In fact, Naldi and her companion were quite wild, and on that occasion in Paris they got both Hitch and Alma completely drunk!

The Mountain Eagle was shot mainly in Munich with locations in the Tyrol (although there are reports that some of the interiors might have been filmed in Paris). To this day, no prints have been found of the film. The script was written by Eliot Stannard, and from what I could gather from the plot found summarized in old movie magazines of the time, the story was quite convoluted. Basically, it was about a woman, Beatrice (Nita Naldi), torn between two men—one, evil and jealous named Pettigrew (Bernard Goetzke), the other, a lonely figure who goes by Fearogod (Malcom Keen) who makes it a mission to protect Beatrice from the fury of Pettigrew. The whole business gets quite dramatic (complete with Fearogod being thrown in jail for a murder that never occurred) but concludes with a happy ending. Unofficially, this could be viewed as the first time my father dealt with one of his favorite themes: a man wrongly accused of a crime. But Daddy was so quick to dismiss the film that I feel it doesn't necessarily qualify as a typical Hitchcock picture. Both my parents knew this one was no winner, and their instincts would be validated when the film would flop at the box office. One bad review sums it all up: "Hitchcock's direction seems to be modeled on German influences, but he cannot find a clear expression of his aim." When *The Mountain Eagle* was completed, Hitch and Alma returned to England—still not married. Hitch needed work (neither *The Pleasure Garden* nor *The Mountain Eagle* had been released yet). More important, Hitch needed a big success and hoped *The Lodger: A Story of the London Fog* would be the film, the breakthrough my parents had been waiting for. It was the first of what my father used to refer to as "a Hitchcock movie."

Hitch had chosen the story himself—a bone-chilling little yarn about a rooming house in which the lodgers gradually begin to suspect that one of them is an insane killer. The film was written by Eliot Stannard, based on the novel by Mrs. Belloc Lowndes (the novel was itself loosely based on the story of Jack the Ripper), and starred Ivor Novello as a mysterious man suspected to be the serial killer of women but who turns out to be innocent.

In *The Lodger*, Alma used to say, Hitch did everything he'd always wanted to do. For instance, he'd never liked inter-titles; he thought they made films slow and unreal, and he used as few cards as possible in *The Lodger*—even though it was a silent picture. Instead, he showed clocks and calendars and newspaper headlines to give facts without ever stopping the action.

The Lodger was the first time that Hitch and Alma were working on one of their own films in England. But there were great problems ahead. *The Lodger* was quite unlike any picture that had ever been made, and both Hitch and Alma knew they would get some resistance from the studio. But when the day dawned for them to see it, Daddy couldn't force himself to go to the studio while it was being screened. It was probably the most suspenseful day in his life—and the most miserable one. Before and during the screening, Hitch and Alma walked about the city aimlessly—seeing nothing and saying nothing—for several hours.

Suddenly, Hitch stopped and looked at his watch. "They've seen it," he said. "Let's go back." Hitch and Alma found a taxi and sped to the studio. They hurried up the stairs and into the production room. There was no need to even ask the question. They looked silently to the faces and read the word "awful" before anyone spoke it. The film was put into a can and set up on a shelf. Alfred Hitchcock's career as a director seemed to be over before it had begun.

∽

NEEDLESS TO SAY, with the fiasco of *The Lodger*, Alma and Hitch needed a distraction—and they chose a rather big one as they decided to finally exchange vows and rings on December 2, 1926, in the Church of the Oratory, in Knightsbridge,

"according to the Rites and Ceremonies of the Catholic Church." Both families were in attendance; Eva, my mother's sister, was Alma's maid of honor, and Will Hitchcock, my father's brother, his best man. After the morning ceremony, a small reception was held at my parents' new flat at 153 Cromwell Road in Earls Court, Knightsbridge, near the Ashburn gardens. (My mother was born a Protestant but converted to Roman Catholism; Alma was baptized on May 31, 1927, received the first Holy Communion on June 1, and was confirmed on June 5 by His Eminence Cardinal Bourne at Westminster Abbey.)

After the ceremony, the reception, and a lunch in the West End, my parents took the boat train to France for their honeymoon. They stopped in Paris and visited Nita Naldi and her elderly companion for a few drinks (that's the time Hitch and Alma drank too much). They then took the train to St. Moritz, Switzerland, and stayed at the Palace Hotel, which became one of their favorite destinations. Originally a place mostly known for its healing waters, St. Moritz became a spot for tourists and celebrities (such as Charles Chaplin, Douglas Fairbanks, and Gloria Swanson) in the twenties. In later years, I spent many of my holidays with my parents there; my father liked to stay inside and read while my mother and I went out skiing—not very well, I must admit. After I was married, my husband, Joe, and our three daughters would join my parents at St. Moritz for Christmas. Those moments in St. Moritz were probably among the fondest memories I have, although I do remember one time we had quite an ordeal getting there—we got on the wrong train, and when we finally reached our destination, our luggage was lost. Daddy was very frustrated—he hated it when things did not go according to his plans. It gave him migraines. But Alma was always there, as the mediator, coming up with solutions. St. Moritz was just simply luxurious, and it was also an opportunity for my parents to socialize with some of their old friends and colleagues like Marlene Dietrich.

～

AFTER SPENDING AN amazing and memorable time at the Palace Hotel, Hitch and Alma returned to London and lived in the top flat at 153 Cromwell Road in West London. It would be our family home until our move to America in 1939. For several months now, *The Lodger* had gathered dust on the studio shelf. And then, simply because a great deal of money had been spent in making it, it was released—apologetically—to a few obscure London cinemas. The public saw it, and the word got out. Quickly, *The Lodger* became known as the best British film that had ever been made and would be *remade* several times, including one version by Alma's old boss, Maurice Elvey, in 1932, also starring Ivor Novello. Daddy would also direct a radio production of *The Lodger* in 1940. I can only imagine how relieved both Alma and Hitch must have been when *The Lodger*

St. Moritz was a favorite vacation spot
for my parents and their friends.

was not only released but acknowledged as a masterpiece. During the difficult time prior to the release of the film, Alma and Hitch got great support from Michael Balcon, the film's producer, and from a man named Ivor Montagu, who would work on several more of my father's pictures. Montagu was one of the founding members of London's Film Society in 1925 and was brought in to help with the editing and titling of *The Lodger* after C. M. Woolf, the distributor, had decided to shelve the picture. He was, for instance, responsible for bringing in artist E. McKnight Kauffer to do title graphics for the film. Woolf was not a popular name in the Hitchcock household, because he was responsible for holding distribution on both *The Pleasure Garden* and *The Lodger*. Unfortunately, this would not be the last time my parents would have to deal with him.

But for now, things were looking up for the young couple. Both were extremely successful and were starting to become quite well-known and respected. One of the perks of making films that both Alma and Hitch enjoyed was that they got to travel all over Europe. And in February 1927, when Mama was asked by British reporter Joan Weston Edwards (for an article titled "Making Good in the Film Trade") what the key to success in film was, Mama had a very simple answer: "Be interested." Alma believed in complete dedication to one's work. She lived for her career, and it was a happy coincidence that Hitch felt the same way.

A PRODUCTIVE COUPLE

$\mathcal{B}$Y NOW, HITCH and Alma had made quite a few friends in the business. One of them was Sidney Bernstein who, despite his strong political views (my parents were completely nonpolitical and remained so even after they moved to America), became very close to Alma and Hitch. Bernstein was quite a figure in British films (he would establish the Granada chain of theaters in 1930 and would eventually form Transatlantic Pictures with my father) and was a real lover of the cinema. Like Ivor Montagu, he was also one of the founders of the Film Society, where Alma and Hitch would befriend other future collaborators and colleagues—among them was director Adrian Brunel with whom Alma would work on a film entitled *The Constant Nymph*. The script (based on the novel and the play of the same title by Margaret Kennedy) was adapted by Margaret Kennedy and Basil Dean. (Dean would also supervise Brunel's directing and would eventually direct one of the two remakes of the film in 1933. The second remake would be made by Warner Brothers exactly ten years later with Charles Boyer and Joan Fontaine.) Alma was in charge of continuity during filming (portions were filmed near Innsbruck and in London). The film starred Ivor Novello as a composer who is married to a domineering wife (Mary Clare) and falls in love with a younger woman played by Mabel Poulton. When the composer finally breaks away from his failed marriage and runs away with the young woman, she falls dead from heart failure. The film also starred Elsa Lanchester in a small role. Lanchester would also later become the bride in *The Bride of Frankenstein* (1935). *The Constant Nymph* was released in London on February 28, 1928, and became one of the most popular films of the twenties. Believed to have been lost for fifty years, a print of the film was discovered in 1995 by film historian Kevin Brownlow. Another British classic had been saved. Mama kept a copy of the script. Several copies had been made, and hers was number three. I still have it and recently discovered that the cover page of the screenplay read *The Constant Nymph,* scenario by Alma Reville. (Incidentally, Alma never changed her last name even after her marriage to Daddy, because she was already professionally established as Alma Reville. She wanted to avoid any confusion.) Alma only received "continuity by" credit on the picture. There was a clear distinction between the synopsis, the treatment, and the scenario (also called shooting script). The scenario was the script, complete with scene number, shot description, and "spoken title." The scenario of *The Constant Nymph* had a total of 505 scenes, and Alma used it on the set as a way to make sure everything was shot and properly matched, hence her credit on the picture, "Continuity by Alma Reville."

Meanwhile, my father's career continued to flourish along-side Alma's, and in 1927, he made four films (with Alma work-ing on only one of them—*The Ring*, for which she did the con-tinuity; otherwise, she was busy on *The Constant Nymph* and was also pregnant with me): *Downhill* was written by Eliot Stannard and based on a play by Ivor Novello and Constance Collier, both writing as David LeStrange (Constance Collier would later star in *Rope* (1948) as the irrestible Mrs. Atwater); *Easy Virtue*, another script by Eliot Stannard, this time from a play by none other than Noel Coward; *The Ring*, written by my father (with some help from Eliot Stannard); and *The Farmer's Wife*, with a screenplay by Stannard based on a play by Eden Phillpotts. The first three films were released in 1927, and *The Farmer's Wife* was released in 1928 (the year I was born). Of the four films, only *The Ring* seemed to resonate (pun intended) with my father.

Hitch would often dismiss some of his earlier work and was his own toughest critic—the same goes for Alma. However, from a completely objective standpoint, when looking at any of those films today, one has to acknowledge Hitch's inventive-ness. Even if the material was not necessarily his cup of tea, he always tried to elevate it to higher ground.

At that point in their careers, I think both of my parents were starving for work. They were growing with the industry and were trying to be as productive as possible. You would say today they were "riding the wave." As for *The Ring*, although it was not a suspense movie, Hitch felt it was his best film since *The Lodger*. Could it be a coincidence that it was the only title of the four that my mother happened to be associated with? *The Ring* was literally about a boxing ring and figuratively about mar-riage and a love triangle. It was Daddy's first film for a new

company called British International Pictures, which was founded in the mid-twenties; my father would make a total of ten films there.

But quite frankly, my parents were at work on another very special production of their own that year: me. With the news that the family would soon get larger, my parents decided to buy a small Tudor country house named Winter's Grace in the village of Shamley Green about 30 miles from London, near Guilford in Surrey, a quaint old-fashioned village surrounded by beautiful scenery. It quickly became a place of peaceful retreat for them, a quiet and remote home to start their family. After they bought the property, my parents referred to it as Shamley Cottage. It was hidden inside the loveliest garden you can imagine. It had small windows, the walls bulged crookedly, and the slates were curling with age. Rock plants graced the roof. The cottage had stood firm since the reign of Henry VII. Only the chimneys gave a hint of the present day. To reach the cottage we had to go through a long, winding lane with trees that formed an archway over the lane.

My parents' home was at the end of the lane. There was a beautiful iron gate inside a brick archway. One day Daddy was trying to work out a difficult part in the plot of a film and distractedly began to draw a gate. He ended up taking the finished design to the village blacksmith on a whim, and it actually became the front gate to the cottage.

It is through the gate that Mama would most often welcome our guests, friends, and family. Those who visited our household in the early days and later on always considered my mother a vivacious and a charming hostess.

When my parents got the place, it was quite small. They eventually decided to add a hall, a master bedroom upstairs, a kitchen, and a dining room. When visiting our home in the thirties, after the renovations had taken place, you would find, upon entering, the cottage hall where my parents liked to throw informal cocktail parties. Oftentimes, Daddy and Mama would bring the cast of their next picture to the cottage and go through the script while entertaining them in the hall.

I remember the living room had a blackened old oak door with a quaint wooden latch that we opened by pulling a bobbin on a string. All the floors in the cottage were completely crooked, and we had to remember to stoop in the right place when we went from one room to another. But in the living room, my parents had kept the plain—and unevenly laid out—tile floor, polished it, and covered it with beautiful Persian rugs. It was in that room that the Tudor style was strongly evident. There was a wonderful oak sideboard on the far wall of the room, where my parents displayed ancient mugs and pewter plates. One of them, I recall, was hammered with the Double Eagle of Imperial Germany. An ancient and beautifully carved oak press ranged under the windows, and a decorative table graced the center of the room.

Dark beams intersected the smooth white plaster of the walls and the ceiling. Easy chairs and a deep sofa provided informal comfort. My favorite aspect of the living room was the deep Tudor fireplace with its red brick and ancient iron blazon with the date 1588.

The kitchen, located next to the living room, was quite modern. My parents did not particularly fancy their meals cooked on a spit! The bathroom was also quite up-to-date, with a porcelain bath, hot rails, a cupboard, and white-tiled walls.

In the living room, there was a door near the fireplace many believed to be a cupboard but instead opened on a tiny staircase. Not only was the staircase alarmingly steep, but it was built on a corner, and the stairs, which sloped from centuries of use, were begging for someone to fall down. It was, of course, part of the charm.

Upstairs, my parents' bedroom had tiny windows, but they were placed on two sides of the room, allowing in plenty of light and air. One detail I remember is that the electric lightswitches were all hidden in the most unlikely places. Occupying the center of the uneven oak floor stood a fine Tudor bed with an elaborately carved headboard. How my parents ever managed to get the bed upstairs is still a mystery to me. Like in the rest of the house, the ceilings had black beams bedded in a cream-colored plaster. On the floor, my parents had Persian rugs and on the bed, a beautiful Indian embroidered bedspread.

There was also an equally quaint and comfortable guest room upstairs which eventually became my bedroom in later years. I remember it had white and blue stars wallpaper.

From my bedroom window, I could see the garden, which had a pond and grass terraces. Hitch and Alma liked working there on summer days because it was always so sunny. It was probably there that, in 1928, they began to work on their next film, *Champagne,* with Hitch adapting an original story by Walter C. Mycroft and Eliot Stannard writing the scenario. It was immediately followed by *The Manxman* in 1929. In later years, Hitch would, again, dismiss those films. According to him, they were only interesting in that they would be his last silent movies. *The Manxman* was adapted from a novel by Sir Hall Caine with a scenario by Eliot Stannard. It was, believe it or not, a remake—there had already been a film made in 1916. Alma was also quite busy that year. She wrote *After the Verdict,* a murder mystery based on a story by Robert Hichens in which a man is wrongly accused of killing a woman who, it turns out, committed suicide; and *The First Born*. Of the two, *The First Born* was the one that seemed worthy of notice. It was a con-voluted and complex period drama about a knight's mistress who tries to convince him that his son is by his wife's lover. The film was directed by Miles Mander, and Alma shared writing credit with him (the film was based on Mander's novel *Oasis* and his play *Those Common People*). Mander also starred with Madeleine Carroll (Alma would be the one to suggest Madeleine to Daddy for the female lead in *The 39 Steps* [1935] and, thus, would begin a close friendship and collaboration), and John Loder (who would star in my father's film *Sabotage* in 1936). With the new house, all those projects, and me on the way, the Hitchcocks were certainly busy and moving fast toward a promising and amazing future.

THE BABY AND THE TALKIES

ALMA LIKED TO say that Hitch actually hated suspense but in real life. The experience they'd had when *The Lodger* was threatened with not being released had been too much for him. Naturally, when I was born on July 7, 1928, Hitch just could not stay in one place. Alma was giving birth at their home on Cromwell Road, as many women did in Britain at the time, and it seemed to be taking too long—perhaps it always seems that way. In any case, Alma could hear Hitch pacing in the living room and finally heard the front door open and close. She knew he had fled. Hitch was gone a long time, and when he came back, Alma had a daughter for him and he had a bracelet for her. "Here," he said, holding it up. "I had to find an excuse to go for a walk."

"It's beautiful," Alma replied. "But you didn't have to go out. I wasn't really feeling bad at all."

"I know you weren't, dear," Daddy said blandly. "But consider my suffering. I nearly died of the suspense."

From that day forward, my father called me "his finest production." My full name was Patricia Alma Hitchcock; I always felt Patricia was a bit too formal, so I liked Pat better. When I got married, I became Pat Hitchcock O'Connell (my maiden name became my middle name). Alma and Hitch would only have one child. I must confess I wish I'd had a brother, but that was simply not in the cards.

We lived in London during the week, and on weekends we would go to our house in the country. I loved our flat in London despite the fact that you had to walk up 96 stairs to get to the upper floor. I remember it was furnished simply, with some

antiques but not a lot of art on the walls. The dining room, which overlooked railroad tracks, was the most important place in the house—we had our meals there, but that was also where my parents worked on their scripts. Because my parents were so active, when I was six months old they hired a nanny named Gladys to take care of me. But Alma spent as much time as she could with me, especially in the afternoons. She would often take me to ride ponies in the park. For my fourth birthday, my parents got me a pony. I named him "Snowball" and kept him in the country. I got an Arabian horse for my eighth birthday. Like Alma, I loved horses. There was no doubt that I loved animals just as much as my parents did. Alma was crazy about dogs, and in the early thirties, she started breeding Wired Haired Terriers. She had about a dozen of them and kept them at Shamley Cottage. Occasionally, she'd take them to shows. By the time we

moved to America, Alma had sold all of her Wire Hairs. We brought with us our two dogs: Edward, an English Cocker Spaniel, and Jenkins, a Sealyham. After they passed on, my parents would get another Sealyham named Johnny. My parents took Johnny everywhere. They would go to their favorite restaurant, Chasen's in Beverly Hills, and would order a filet to bring back to the dog (who stayed in the car with the chauffeur). When I was growing up, we also had an Old English Sheepdog named Scamp. I can clearly picture us back at Shamley Cottage, Daddy smoking a cigar in one corner of the room and Mama brushing the dogs for hours and hours. We were so comfortable and so happy in this very uncomplicated setting.

I was a very easy child, although I do remember one specific time where I decided to be a very naughty girl. Alma and Hitch decided to have my portrait painted, and so, at eight years old, I was sent to an artist named Hilda Kidman. I had to go and stay with her for three weeks. We worked in her studio, and I hated

it so much that I stole the key, locked the door, and hid the key under the carpet. I figured if we couldn't get in, I could go home. But of course, Hilda had another set. My parents wanted this portrait so badly. I had to sit in for a couple hours in the morning and a couple in the afternoon. The artist would eventually paint, not on my recommendation, portraits of Princess Elizabeth and Margaret. I can only hope she had a better time with them than she did with me. But aside from this event, I was pretty well behaved. Early on, I was taught to be very proper and polite when we had visitors—following British custom, I had to curtsy when introduced to a guest of the family. I would teach my daughters to do the same.

～

ALTHOUGH I WAS a bit advanced for my age, movies definitely began talking before I did. That transition would be lucky for some and tragic for others (actors, for instance, who did not speak English properly could obviously get away with it in silent films, but their thick accent and poor delivery became issues with sound pictures). Sound was revolutionizing the industry, and it was only logical (I think) that the first British film to talk be a Hitchcock picture! The title of it was *Blackmail* (1929).

The making of *Blackmail* is an interesting story, one my parents loved to cite as one of the most exciting moments in their career. The film was shot at Elstree Studios and started out as a silent film, but as the production proceeded, a decision was made by John Maxwell, the head of the company, to play the last two reels in sound. During the shooting of the silent part, two small sound stages were being built in another part of the lot. Hitch then conceived the idea of making the film into a full-length talking picture. Without letting the powers that be know about it, Hitch completed the last two reels of the film in sound as planned and then went back and filled in the rest of the picture with dialogue as well.

Because *Blackmail* had started off as a silent picture, it mattered little what kind of voices the actors had. The leading lady in *Blackmail* was a Czech, Anny Ondra, who played in pictures in studios in Berlin, and who had already worked with Hitch on *The Manxman*. However, because she was playing an English girl, her foreign accent was problematic. With the commencement of the talking pictures era, there was no such thing as putting a voice on afterward and there was no effective way of "dubbing" the actors. This was overcome, however, by having an English actress (Joan Barry) sit on the side of the set with her own microphone while Miss Ondra just mouthed the words. It was an extremely difficult job but had the most satisfactory and undetectable result. *Blackmail* would eventually be released in both versions—as a silent film and as a sound picture.

Blackmail was based on a play by Charles Bennet, who would instantly become a very close friend of ours. Charles was like an uncle to me. He would move to Hollywood before us and be one of the friends to welcome us to the land of opportunities. Charles and I stayed in touch until he died in 1995. At the time he passed away, Charles was still writing—and was probably the oldest screenwriter still working actively with the studios. At the time of his death, he had been working on a remake of *Blackmail* for Twentieth Century Fox. It was very exciting for me to see that Charles was trying to keep the Hitchcock flame alive through his many interviews and appearances in seminars and even on television. He never forgot to mention Alma.

Charles did not write the original screenplay for *Blackmail* (Hitch did, with dialogue by Benn Levy), but it was based on his play. After this initial encounter, he would write or co-write with Alma six other Hitchcock movies—some of the best films my parents did in England and one in the States, *Foreign Correspondent* (1940) for which Charles would receive an Academy Award nomination.

Blackmail had all the ingredients of the perfect thriller and showed that my father was as comfortable with sound as he was with silent films. The story was about a young woman (Anny Ondra) who stabs a man to death in self-defense—he was trying to assault her. One clever trick was the repetition of the word "knife," which rises to a scream as Anny Ondra relives the moment of the killing. The film is incredibly suspenseful and climaxes into a chase at the British Museum. This chase sequence is a classic example of yet another aspect of the "Hitchcock touch," as it foreshadows other sequences such as the ones taking place at the Albert Hall in *The Man Who Knew Too Much* (1934 and the remake in 1956), the Statue of Liberty in *Saboteur* (1942), and Mount Rushmore in *North By Northwest* (1959). The film also marked another one of Daddy's cameo appearances. (He had made his first cameo in *The Lodger* because of a shortage of extras.) It was possibly one of his lengthier roles. He can be spotted on a subway, trying to read a book while a little boy is annoying him and trying to grab his hat.

Blackmail was an event when it was released in November 1929 and was advertised as "The First British Talkie!" My parents were in heaven. Critics loved the film, and it put Hitch "on top of the heap," as Michael Powell, the screenwriter/director/producer of many masterpieces, put it. "When the film reached Hollywood," Powell, who was the still photographer on *Champagne, The Manxman,* and *Blackmail,* wrote in his autobiography, "he was deluged with offers. But he wasn't ready to go. Yet." Reviews were amazing and suggested that *Blackmail* was intelligent and clever. The name "Hitchcock" was becoming synonymous with "great cinema."

That same year, Alma also experienced the transition from silent to sound away from Hitch. She worked on a picture that was shot as a silent and had sound added to it one year later. The film was titled *The Romance of Seville,* and was directed by Norman Walker with Alma as co-screenwriter. The story, set in Spain, was about an artist in love with a girl engaged to a jewel thief.

In 1929, Hitch and Alma worked on *Juno and the Paycock,* based on a popular play by Sean O'Casey. (Alma wrote the scenario.) Both Daddy and Mama were not too thrilled with the film, which, they felt, despite the good reviews, was just a filmed play. It didn't offer the great visual and sound opportunities that Hitch had been able to create on *Blackmail.*

For his next effort, Daddy was asked by British International Pictures to contribute along with other directors to a musical revue called *Elstree Calling* (1930). This was, in a few words—my father's own—a completely forgettable experience.

For the next five films following *Elstree Calling,* Alma would collaborate with Hitch on the screenplays. One they were really excited about was *Murder!* based on the play *Enter Sir John* by Clemence Dane (a pseudonym for Winifred Ashton) and Helen Simpson; the adaptation was by Hitch and Walter Mycroft, Alma signed the scenario. It would be the first sound picture for actor Herbert Marshall (who would star as the traitor in my father's *Foreign Correspondent* a few years later). *Murder!* was the story of a woman wrongly accused of murdering a man. She goes on trial; on the jury sits Sir John, a famous producer/director played by Marshall. He doesn't believe she is guilty, and he starts his own investigation (he has, of course, fallen in love with the accused woman). It turns out that the real killer is a man revealed to be a transvestite. The girl is freed and ends up with Sir John, who helped her out of jail and always believed in her innocence. The film, although a bit long and not as engrossing as *Blackmail,* was full of clever visual and audio innovations. For instance, Daddy wanted Sir John to be listening to the radio while shaving, but since films could not be dubbed in those days, he had to have a small live orchestra play the score on the set while he filmed the actor! One sequence early on in the picture showed a couple meeting Sir John. The man in the couple has to walk toward Sir John, and Daddy wanted to convey the idea that the man was intimidated. His solution was simple: He threw down a carpet (over a mattress, I believe), and had the actor walk unsteadily over it. In that single insert shot, the audience understood literally that the character was hesitant in his approach toward Sir John. *Murder* was a "whodunit"—not necessarily my parents' favorite type of mystery, but it was definitely a successful attempt. An interesting side: my father also shot a German version of the film with German actors under the title *Mary.*

Hitch and Alma were unstoppable. They were simply making one film after another. They would keep up that pace pretty much through the end of their long and successful lives and careers. Alma and Hitch would next work on a remake of *The Skin Game* (1931; the original was made in 1920). Hitch adapted the play by John Galsworthy, and Alma wrote the scenario. Daddy always claimed he didn't do this film by choice. He was, you could say, a "director for hire." Nonetheless, the film co-starred Edmund Gwenn, who would be featured in several Hitchcock films, including one of my parents' favorites, *The Trouble with Harry,* in 1955.

Despite all their work, my parents knew how to have a good time. They did not go out a lot, but they loved to travel. I was three and a half years old when Daddy decided to take us on a cruise. We went to Africa and to the Caribbean when I was four years old. My parents had great appreciation for different cultures. The only thing I remember about the trip to Africa was that, on the ship, when we passed the Equator, there was a ceremony where a passenger would end up being thrown in the pool. That was the part of the trip where the Hitchcock couple was hiding, not in their cabin, but behind their home movie camera, and captured the entire ritual on film, thus guaranteeing that they would not end up in the pool fully clothed. Alma and Hitch loved that trip.

It was no coincidence, given Alma and Hitch's love for traveling, that they chose to make the film *Rich and Strange* (released in the States as *East of Shanghai*) in 1931. (It would be released in 1932.) Alma co-wrote the scenario with Val Valentine, based on a novel by Dale Collins. It was the story of a couple who wins money and decides to take a trip around the world. Mama and Daddy definitely could identify, and when Hitch decided there should be a scene in the picture that took place at the Folies Bergères in Paris, they both went there for a visit. At one point, Daddy innocently asked a man if they could see some belly dancing—that was also part of the research. The man took them down to the street to a cab and said, "It's in the annex." Hitch and Alma soon realized they were on their way to a brothel! But they were curious and went in. In front of Alma, the madam asked Hitch whether he would like one of the young ladies. Needless to say, my parents tore out of there

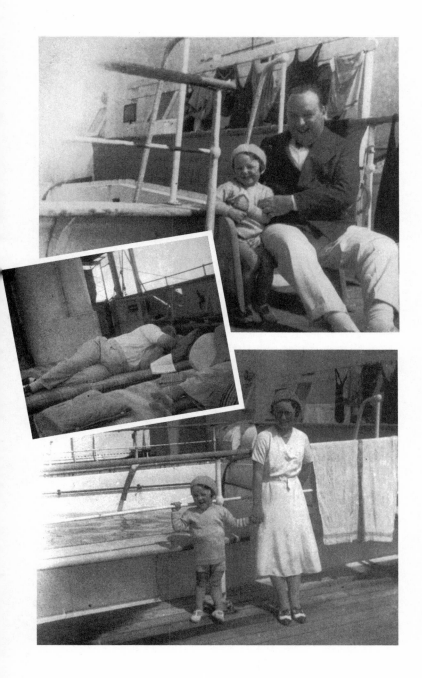

fast, but the essence of that experience, along with others, found their way into *Rich and Strange*. The cast included Henry Kendall, Joan Barrie (who had dubbed "live on the set" the voice of Anny Ondra in *Blackmail*), and Elsie Randolph (who would star many years later in *Frenzy*). Elsie Randolph became a good friend and visited us at Shamley Cottage on several occasions.

After *Rich and Strange*, Alma and Hitch worked on a very unsuccessful film called *Number Seventeen*. The scenario was by Alma, Hitch, and Rodney Ackland, based on a play by J. Jefferson Farjeon. There had been a version done in Germany in 1928. I personally think it's a very interesting picture. Although it isn't as obvious as it would be in later pictures such as *The 39 Steps, Number Seventeen* introduced the notion of the MacGuffin. The actual term was something that originated from screenwriter Angus MacPhail—the MacGuffin was used to trap lions in the Scottish Highlands. Since there are no lions in the Scottish Highlands, the MacGuffin is irrelevant. As explained by my father, the MacGuffin is what drives the story, but the audience doesn't really need to know what it is. In this case, it is a stolen necklace. We never find out its origin or any details about it, other than it's what the bad guys are after. Another bizarre detail in the film has to do with one of the female characters who is introduced as being deaf and mute. At the end, and without any explanation, she starts talking. I think Hitch and Alma might have been testing the audience—how much could they get away with while avoiding explaining too much. That was an art, one that Hitch perfected over the years. The story of *Number Seventeen* mainly took place in an abandoned house, but the climax had an exciting chase and an impressive train wreck, completely done with miniatures, which started my father's fascination with trains (featured in a good number of his films) but also, and most important, displayed his talent as an action director.

Alma also continued to work on non-Hitchcock films. One of them was *Sally in Our Alley* (1931), which she co-wrote with Miles Malleson and Archie Pitt. The film was directed by her old boss, Maurice Elvey. "A formula picture all the way and not a good one," said *Variety* at the time. Alma also co-wrote, from the stage play by Dorothy Brandon, *The Outsider,* starring Joan Barrie. The story was about the daughter of a leading surgeon crippled from birth, who is eventually cured by an unqualified osteopath (described as a "quack doctor" in the 1931 reviews). In 1932, Alma would co-write *The Water Gypsies,* based on a novel by A. P. Herbert, starring Ann Todd (who would later appear in my parents' *The Paradine Case* in 1947) and *Nine Till Six,* based on a play by Aimee and Philip Stuart. Both were romance stories.

Hitch also played solo, this time as the producer of *Lord Camber's Ladies,* directed by Benn W. Levy (the playwright and stage director who had worked on *Blackmail*), starring Gertrude Lawrence, Sir Gerald du Maurier (in my parents' opinion, the world's greatest actor of his time), and Nigel Bruce (who would star in *Rebecca* in 1940 and *Suspicion* in 1941). It wasn't a very enjoyable experience, except for the fact that Hitch was working with Gerald du Maurier. They were both extremely funny and would pull stunts on each other all the time, one always trying to "outjoke" the other. One day, my father had a big horse put in du Maurier's dressing room while he was onstage. After the performance, du Maurier opened his door, saw the horse, and said, "Hello there, old boy!" The two of them would just go back and forth. Alma always went along with it, though it was Daddy who was always the instigator, never she—but she loved it nonetheless! My father had an incredible sense of humor. He would often say, "If you couldn't look at something and see the humor in it, then you missed everything." I was aware of his sense of humor as far back as I can remember. He liked physical humor and telling jokes, but most of all, he loved to play practical jokes. Despite what certain biographies might have reported, Daddy's sense of humor was never cruel. He was the kindest person living.

In 1933, Hitch and Alma worked on a film titled *Waltzes from Vienna*. Alma wrote the scenario with Guy Bolton, who was also the author of the play of the same title. It was a period film and "a musical without music," as my father put it. I think at the time, Hitch was really at a crossroad—he had had some success with films like *The Lodger* and *Blackmail*, but he had had some failures as well. Hitch and Alma were working a lot. With Alma's help and support, Hitch was in search of affirming his identity as a filmmaker. And together, they would soon become the couple "who knew so much."

A NEW BEGINNING

*T*HE VERY SMART and prescient man Michael Balcon, who had given my father the opportunity to direct his first film *The Pleasure Garden,* was now with Gaumont British and asked Hitch to do a film called *The Man Who Knew Too Much*. Around that time, my father had been developing a project based on the Bulldog Drummond stories with Charles Bennett (author of the play *Blackmail*). Bulldog Drummond was kind of an amateur James Bond. One of his stories involved international spying and the kidnapping of a baby. Ultimately, that project fell through, but the frame of that particular story became the basis of the *The Man Who Knew Too Much* script, a film that would solidly shape my father's reputation both in England and in America. Later, I learned elements in the story had been brewing in the back of Hitch's mind ever since he and Alma had honeymooned in Saint Moritz, a locale our family enthusiastically returned to often. At the Grand Hotel, Hitch had told Alma that he would love to create a picture featuring a skating rink with a man tracing numbers on the ice that would turn out to be espionage code. That specific scene with the ice-skating rink was never realized, but Hitch did set the opening of the film in Saint Moritz, where a young couple, Jill and Bob Lawrence (played by Leslie Banks and Edna Best) and their young daughter (Nova Pilbeam) meet a French man (Pierre Fresnay) who is a spy. The Frenchman is shot on the dance floor, but before he dies, he reveals to the couple that a murder is to happen in London. Subsequently, the daughter is kidnapped and the couple returns to London. The climactic sequence takes place during a concert at Albert Hall, where the murder is to take place at the crash of the cymbals. Jill screams, interrupting the concert and thus preventing the crime. This is one of the films in which considerable activity and conflict lead to a happy ending; the villains are stopped and the little girl is reunited with her parents.

Although Alma did not receive credit on the film, she was present and took part in the story conferences that were held at my parents' home on Cromwell Road. (The writing credits read: *The Man Who Knew Too Much* by Charles Bennett, D. B. Wyndham Lewis, scenario by Edwin Greenwood and A. R. Rawlinson with additional dialogue by Emlyn Williams.) One of the most inspired pieces of casting in the film was Peter Lorre, who played the head of the spy ring. *The Man Who Knew Too Much* was his first British role—I was too young to remember him clearly—but Alma once told me his nickname was "The Long Overcoat" because he always wore an overcoat that came down to his feet. The role called for Lorre to have a scar on his face, and apparently one day he announced he was getting married. But shooting had to go on, and Peter ended up having to rush to his own wedding ceremony in full makeup!

Peter and my parents were good friends, and he worked again with them a few years later on *Secret Agent* in 1936.

The Man Who Knew Too Much put Daddy in top form. Alma never failed to point out the clever stuff Daddy did in his films, and *The Man Who Knew Too Much* was no exception; it is full of interesting visuals that were regarded as groundbreaking at the time. For instance, when the Frenchman Louis Bernard is killed, he is actually dancing with Jill; her jealous husband had tugged on the man's jacket, which unravels (symbolically and literally). Visually it is amusing, and the audience is laughing, then is shocked when suddenly the man is shot. On second viewing, you realize that the unraveling of the jacket symbolically tells us that the man's life is hanging by a thread! I'm not one to analyze my father's pictures, but I couldn't help noting that one.

There are a lot of other classic moments in the film. One of them takes place at a dentist office, which the spies use as a front for their operations. Originally, Hitch had wanted to set the scene in a barber shop—he liked the visual possibilities of men with hot towels covering their face—but director Mervyn LeRoy had already used that idea for a key sequence in his film *I Am a Fugitive from a Chain Gang* (1932). So Daddy went with the dentist office instead. The "pièce de résistance" was the sequence at Albert Hall—which was, in fact, shot on a soundstage using the special visual process called Shuftan. The idea of the single crash of the cymbals as the cue for the killer to shoot his gun was apparently inspired by a comic strip that had appeared in a satirical magazine called *Punch*. It showed a little man (known as "the one note man") in his routine, getting up, going to work, doing a single note with his cymbals, then going back home.

The climax of the film, when the police are surrounding the building where the spies are hiding, was based on a real incident—the Sidney Street siege, which took place in 1910. In real life, the police were trying to arrest a group of anarchists but had to get help from the army (the operation was headed by

Winston Churchill). The film censors were concerned with the way Daddy was planning on depicting the event in his film, and they wouldn't allow him to show policemen carrying weapons (Bobbies are not allowed to carry guns) and even suggested that the spies be stopped using fire hoses (something Churchill had himself suggested during the real event). Eventually, Hitch got away with showing the arrival of a truck from which rifles were handed out to the police.

The Man Who Knew Too Much was a pivotal film for my parents. It was a turning point, although at first, it seemed they were reliving the awful situation of *The Lodger,* involving yet again the now-head of distribution at Gaumont British, C. M. Woolf. Woolf obviously resented my father and while Michael Balcon was out of town, he screened the film and simply hated it. He even suggested hiring another director to recut the picture. Hitch and Alma were once again devastated. This was like déjà vu. My father was extremely depressed and, to clear his mind, decided to start adapting, with Charles Bennett, the classic spy novel by John Buchan *The 39 Steps* while awaiting the fate of *The Man Who Knew Too Much.*

That same year, Alma co-wrote the adaptation of a novel by Dennis Wheatley titled *Forbidden Territory;* the film was directed by Phil Rosen. The plot: A young Englishman goes to Russia to recover some buried crown jewels and lands in forbidden territories, where a fleet of planes are being built. He is sent to jail. His father and brother go to Moscow looking for him and are helped by a Russian singer. "They are immediately placed under the severest espionage," wrote *Variety,* "and the ingenuity exercised in surmounting this results in intensely absorbing melodramatic situations that lift the picture far above the commonplace." The film was released on October 19, 1934, and the good notices were encouraging.

As for *The Man Who Knew Too Much,* things started looking up a bit when Ivor Montagu, the film's associate producer and the man who had also helped so much on *The Lodger*, convinced Woolf to screen the picture to the trades. The response was amazing, and Woolf agreed to finally release the film to great reviews. It was a success in England and in America, where it made the *New York Times* top ten list of the best films of 1935 (the film came out in England in December 1934) and caught the attention of producer David O. Selznick, among others. At that time, there were already discussions of remaking the film in an American setting, but that idea would not really come to fruition until 1956, when my father decided to do the remake himself at Paramount.

~

ALMA WOULD ONLY do one more non-Hitchcock film prior to our move to America in 1939; she co-adapted a picture called *The Passing of the Third Floor Back* (1936), based on a famous play by Jerome K. Jerome. The story strangely resembled the set-up of *The Lodger*; a "stranger," played by the amazing actor Conrad Veidt, takes a room on the third floor of a London rooming house and changes the lives of the other tenants. The *Variety* review pointed out the powerful acting, the directing by Berthold Viertel, and added: ". . . responsible for putting lots of tang into Jerome's mellowed theme are the adaptators." As satisfying as those good notices must have been for my mother, she preferred working with Daddy, and he liked having her around. After the encouraging response to *The Man Who Knew Too Much*, Alma (under the credit "Continuity") would collaborate with Hitch on his next five films—without a doubt, the best of his British pictures: *The 39 Steps* (1935), *Secret Agent* (1936), *Sabotage* (1936), *Young and Innocent* (1938), and *The Lady Vanishes* (1938). All but *The Lady Vanishes* were written or co-written by Charles Bennett. By the time they were working on *Young and Innocent*, Charles would move to America.

Vaguely similar to the title character of *The Lodger*, *The 39 Steps* was about a man wrongly accused of murder. It was based on the novel by John Buchan, adapted by Charles Bennett, dialogue by Ian Hay, and, as with *The Man Who Knew Too Much,* continuity by Alma. The man, Richard Hannay (played by the very talented Robert Donat), has to escape from the police and travel through Scotland in pursuit of a spy ring to prove his innocence. Along the way and through bizarre circumstances, he is literally hand-cuffed to a woman (a blonde played Madeleine Carroll) who at first thinks he is guilty but slowly realizes that not only is he inno-cent, but she has fallen in love with him. One of my favorite sequences takes place at the end of the film when Hannay sud-denly realizes that an entertainer named Mr. Memory has the information wanted by the spies in his head. That part of the plot is what my father referred to as the MacGuffin, which I men-tioned in connection to *Number Seventeen.* The MacGufffin in this case is what the villains are after but we don't really know what it is. We get a vague sense of it, but that's all. There was a MacGuffin in *North by Northwest,* for instance—the spy played by James Mason carries microfilm inside a statuette. It's obviously secret information he is intending to sell, but we never find out what it really is because it's irrelevant. Alma loved *The 39 Steps.* She would work with Daddy in the sixties on the adaptation of another Richard Hannay adventure titled *Three Hostages.* Unfortunately, the project was never realized.

When Daddy began working on *The 39 Steps,* he decided it was time to hire a secretary. Joan Harrison was last in the line of applicants. By the time he got to her, it was around lunchtime and Daddy was starving, so he simply asked her, "Do you speak German?" She said she didn't, and that was the extent of the interview. "You're hired," my father told the blue-eyed woman standing in front of him. Joan admitted that Hitch taught her everything she knew about motion pictures. Every minute she was with him, she was absorbing and learning. Joan got her first screenwriting credit on my father's film *Jamaica Inn* in 1939. There was no doubt the lady was special, and she instantly

Daddy, Joan Harrison, and Mama.

became part of the Alma and Hitch team. Both Daddy and Mama adored her and had no hesitation in inviting her to follow us when we moved to America. Joan continued to write and collaborate with my parents for several years and then became a producer in her own right. One of my favorite films of hers was a film noir called *Phantom Lady* (1944), directed by Robert Siodmak and based on a book by Cornell Woolrich (the author of *Rear Window*). In 1955, Daddy lured Joan back to produce his television series, *Alfred Hitchcock Presents*. It was on one of the shows that she met author Eric Ambler. They were married shortly after Ambler was divorced from his first wife. My parents were among the few to attend the ceremony. Born in Guildford, Surrey, England, on June 20, 1911, Joan died in London on August 14, 1994. She was 83. Joan was one of the women who Hitch persevered to promote in film in the early days. Alma was very supportive of that, too; she and Joan were very close and loved working on scripts together. Hitch's dedication and reliance on women was thoroughly recognized by him, and he remained devoted and grateful to them.

BEFORE THE MOVE

ITCH HAD CERTAINLY become a celebrity in England, but frankly, I was unaware of most of his prominence. Alma was steadfast that we maintain our normal family life, and at school, no one ever mentioned any of my parents' pictures. Born to the film business was not as glamorous as it became when we moved to Hollywood, and I don't really remember attending any fancy premieres or parties in London. I imagine it was unusual that my parents let me watch their films freely at an early age, even though some of them were a bit violent. In *The 39 Steps,* for instance, a woman is stabbed in the back and falls over actor Robert Donat at the beginning of the film. That was quite shocking at the time, but my parents always made it clear to me that "It's only a movie." They would let me see anything creative they were involved in. However, I must confess I was more drawn to stage musicals than I was to movies. What my father did for a living only became notable to me later on in his career. What seemed to be a bigger deal from my perspective was the fact that my mother worked. My friends' mothers stayed at home; that was very much the norm at that time. But because Alma was in such an innovative industry, none of my friends could really comprehend what she actually did. My daughters never knew that their Grandmother Alma had worked at such an early age in the film business until they were much older. To them, it was an enlightening and inspiring discovery because they were very much aware of the woman's liberation movement when they were growing up. Quite unexpectedly, Alma became an example for them to follow, a role model within their own family.

As Hitch and Alma's careers continued to escalate, social engagements were plentiful. I would always accompany them. I became aware as I got older that my parents were never judgmental of others; a quality I admire to this day. However, proper manners were very important to both of them. When I became a mother, I relied on Alma to teach my daughters what she had taught me. Mary, my eldest, remembers: "My grandmother was a classic woman. She and my mother taught my sisters and I manners such as wearing gloves and how to behave in certain places. Our lifestyle within our own home was very relaxed, however, with lots of kids, dogs, and friends running around and dropping in. When we were with Grandma, we learned quickly what was acceptable behavior." I wouldn't say that my daughters were at all scared of Alma, but they certainly could tell when she was not happy with them. They respected and loved her so much that her disapproval would cause them great distress. I trust Alma knew she had that kind of influence over them—she never abused it with me, my daughters, or even my father. My mother was definitely someone you did not want to cross or betray or even disappoint. We respected her too much. My father, I think, was more accepting and forgiving; he saw things with a lot of humor.

Both of my parents were always dressed impeccably. Hitch was notorious for wearing a suit and tie, even on the set. I was once told a funny story about my father. A young man once approached him, introduced himself, and said he was a director. My father looked at him and saw he had an open shirt and replied, "Real directors wear ties."

Hitch's involvement with wardrobe is obvious from watching his films, but it extended to my mother's own wardrobe as

Mama, wearing one of her typical pantsuit outfits, standing next to her sister Aunt Eveline.

well. In the thirties, he had men's suits made for her by a famous tailor named Austin Read in London. I remember my mother telling me that one day they checked into a hotel and my mother was dressed in pants—I guess it was considered racy to do that then and quite provocative. They walked down to the desk to register, and my father noticed two women whispering to one another and pointing at Alma's outfit. So Hitch turned to his wife and, in a very loud voice as though she was deaf, said, "Alma, do you see those two ladies? They're talking about your trousers!" My mother just jumped but Daddy continued, "Didn't you hear what I said?" He loved to shock people.

But beautiful clothes and the latest fashion were essential in his films as well—sometimes, they were even part of the plot. In *Rear Window* (1954), Grace Kelly works in the world of fashion and is always wearing the latest thing; in *Vertigo* (1958), the character played by Jimmy Stewart is obsessed with recreating the look of a woman he lost; and in *To Catch a Thief* (1955), the climax of the film takes place during a fancy costume ball. Hitch's enduring collaboration with costume designer Edith Head (who also designed clothes for Alma) was not only legendary but as important as his work with the actors, the cameraman, and the editor.

Interestingly, although Daddy loved the latest fashion for his stars, he confined himself to conservative wear. In the early seventies, we—my parents, my husband, and my daughters—all went on a vacation to Hawaii. My father only ever wore white shirts, and Alma had bought him a mint green shirt for the trip. He came down to the beach in that shirt, and my daughter Mary said to him, "Where did you get *that*?" We were all so shocked to see him wearing a color! He replied, "Your grandmother bought it for me." I think he was only wearing it because he didn't want to hurt her feelings. I always wondered if Mama had tried to pull a prank on my father by giving him that shirt!

The truth is, Daddy was a man who liked the familiar, especially when it came to the way he dressed. "Hitch's affinity for

Mama and costume designer Edith Head.

a pet routine carries over into his wardrobe," Mama used to tell our friends, and she was right. Each day of the year, he wore exactly the same type of clothes: a dark blue suit, tailored by the same man who had been doing it for eons; a dark blue tie; a white shirt; black socks; and black shoes. He rarely wore a hat or a coat, no matter how far north he traveled. It was almost impossible to find a piece of lint on a Hitchcock suit or a smudge on his shoes because he was the tidiest man on Earth. In all the years my parents were married, Alma never knew him to leave a toothbrush or a tube of shaving cream out of place or to ever walk out of a lavatory without making sure the washbowl was immaculate.

BUT BETWEEN 1935 and 1938, there was no time to think about clothing and wardrobe; Alma and Hitch were way too busy making movies. To this day, I still wonder how they managed to do five important films in those three years. It was, I believe, only possible because of their collaboration.

The first of the five films was *Secret Agent* (1936), which reunited my parents with Peter Lorre and Madeleine Carroll. A young John Gielgud played the hero, a man named Ashenden, and the film, written by Charles Bennett with dialogue by Ian Hay and Jesse Lasky Jr. doing additional dialogue, combined stories by W. Somerset Maugham ("The Traitor" and "The Hairless Mexican") and a play by Campbell Dixon (the play was based on the stories). Although not as memorable as *The 39 Steps, Secret Agent* was an interesting and cruel concept: An intelligence agent is assigned to go to Switzerland to kill a spy and mistakenly gets rid of an innocent tourist—the real spy is killed later during a thrilling train wreck sequence (my father's second since *Number Seventeen*). One of the twists in the story was that the villain was almost more charming than the hero.

An Agatha Christie–type character in Hitch's *Suspicion* (Alma co-wrote the script), says about the villains in her mystery novels: "I always think of my murderers as my heroes." This quote from the film parallels my father's own treatment of the bad guys in his films. He always made his villains charming and polite. According to Hitch, it was a mistake to think that if you put a villain on the screen, he must sneer nastily, stroke his black mustache, or kick a dog. Some of the most famous murderers in criminology were real charmers, and the really frightening thing about Hitchcock villains is their surface likeableness. Daddy, as Mama pointed out on many occasions even to me, was a master at making his killers as appealing as his heroes. They had to have a cynical sense of humor, and although their view of the world is sinister, it had to seem somewhat amusing to the audience.

What I enjoyed most in *Secret Agent* was the relationship between Madeleine Carroll and John Gielgud. They have to pretend to be married, and some of their scenes together are hilarious. There is another interesting sequence in the film that takes place in a chocolate factory—because the film is set in Switzerland, it was only logical to use the local industry as part of the backdrop. My father always tried to maximize the use of his locations.

Sabotage (1936), which my parents did next, was written by Charles Bennett, based on a novel by Joseph Conrad called *Secret Agent* with dialogue by Ian Hay, Helen Simpson, and E.V. H. Emmett doing additional dialogue. The film starred an American actress, Sylvia Sidney. Her creepy husband was played by Oscar Homolka. I like the film very much, although, like my parents, I deplore the fact that a child is killed in one of the most surprising sequences ever filmed by my father. Homolka is a saboteur who is unable to deliver a time bomb, so he wraps it up and asks his wife's brother, a young boy, to deliver it instead. The boy doesn't know what the package contains and gets distracted along the way. He gets on a bus, and the bomb explodes.

The boy's sister has her revenge and kills her husband at the end. The killing of the remorseful husband had to seem almost like a suicide, but it had to be performed by his wife so that the audience would not lose sympathy for her. It was a challenge getting it right, but it worked beautifully. Yet the film was definitely a bit of a downer. *Sabotage* remains, probably with *Vertigo* and *Psycho,* one of my father's darkest films, where a happy ending was impossible.

~∂

BY THE TIME I was nine years old, I spent more time at the theater than I did at the movies. A highlight was when my parents took me to *Careless Rapture,* a musical starring Ivor Novello. I would see *everything* that Novello starred in. He and my parents had remained good friends, and he would always get us a private box. I also remember my father falling asleep during one of the performances. During intermission, Novello had a note brought to Daddy that said: "Of all the people seeing this show, you seem to be enjoying it the least!" Alma thought it was very funny. Daddy was not amused.

In 1936, Hitch took us (Alma and I) and his mother to Naples. Mama, as customary each time she went to Naples, stayed in bed with strep throat. And as always, she did not complain and refused to let it spoil the trip. Daddy, Grandma, and I had fun visiting Capri and the Blue Grotto. At one point, Grandma refused to climb aboard a small rowboat. She and Daddy argued and argued about it; they both could be quite stubborn.

Back home, Hitch and Alma immediately got on with a film called *Young and Innocent* (1937), based on the novel *A Shilling for Candles* by Josephine Tey. Charles Bennett was one of the screenwriters, along with Edwin Greenwood, Anthony Armstrong, and Gerald Savory doing dialogue. The story was about a young man (Derrick de Marney) wrongly accused of murdering a woman. We know that the real killer has a nervous twitch in his eyes and that he plays drums in a band. At the end, in the climactic scene before the killer is finally caught, the camera descends on a group of dancers, to the bandstand, and ends on the man twitching. That scene alone made a huge impression on me—and audiences. The film also starred Nova Pilbeam, the little girl from *The Man Who Knew Too Much,* who was by now a beautiful young woman. *Young and Innocent* had the right blend of action, humor, and Hitchcockian touches.

Because Hitch was settling in such specific genre, his films became more memorable. It was inevitable, then, that sooner or later, my parents would be called to move to America. They had received several offers (from RKO and MGM), and my father had made a brief trip to America in 1937. We would officially move two years later, after Daddy completed two more films in England: one of his best, *The Lady Vanishes* (1938), followed by one of my least favorite, *Jamaica Inn* (1939).

Based on the novel *The Wheel Spins* by Ethel Lina White and written by Sidney Gilliatt and Frank Launder, *The Lady Vanishes* is right up there with some of my father's best films. The story takes place almost exclusively on a train. An old lady (played by Dame May Whitty) disappears, and everyone, except the heroine (Margaret Lockwood), denies ever seeing her onboard. I have great memories of visiting the set; the film was almost entirely shot on a sound stage at Islington Studios. It was quite a small stage (only 90 feet long), so I was very impressed when I saw they had managed to build the interior of a train compartment. It was then, and still is, quite realistic onscreen. The actors were all very nice to me, especially Margaret Lockwood, who was an amazing and respected actress. My parents simply loved her.

While *The Lady Vanishes* was being completed, my father received word from Myron Selznick, brother of producer David O. Selznick (Myron Selznick was one of the biggest talent agents and was Daddy's agent). They had met in 1924 on the set of *The Passionate Adventure.* Myron asked whether Hitch would be able to come to Hollywood to make a film about the *Titanic* for David O. Selznick. Because he was at the end of his contract with Gaumont British, Hitch became very intrigued by the offer. Alma was not only thrilled, she was proud. In August 1937, Alma and Hitch went to New York for ten days. They were met by Kay Brown, who was Selznick's New York representative. Hitch and Alma also met Jock Whitney, who was in partnership with Selznick, and in between business conversations, they went to the races in Saratoga. My parents then returned to London to complete the editing on *The Lady Vanishes.* In July 1938, Hitch and Alma went to Hollywood for the first time; the objective was to consummate the Selznick deal. The contract was for seven years, the first film firm, and the subsequent years optional (the first film had to be a Selznick film; but then Hitch could be "on loan" to other studios). Alma and Hitch absolutely loved California—particularly the weather. They were convinced they could have a comfortable life in Hollywood. And they felt I would be happy and prosper there as well. Upon returning to London, Hitch got to work on the *Titanic* film. Selznick would eventually abandon the idea and substitute Hitch's first movie in America with *Rebecca,* based on the novel by Daphne du Maurier.

David O. Selznick's instinct on Hitch's appeal to American audiences was right on the mark and was confirmed when *The Lady Vanishes* received the New York Critic's Award for Best Film of 1938. The movie was, of course, a huge hit in England as well.

By pure coincidence, Daddy's last film in England before we left for America was also be based on a novel by Daphne du Maurier (daughter of Hitch and Alma's good friend Gerald du Maurier) with a screenplay by Sidney Gilliatt and Joan Harrison and dialogue by Gilliatt. *Jamaica Inn* starred Charles Laughton (who was also one of the producers) and Maureen O'Hara. It was a period shipwreck story set on the Cornish Coast that did not really work. Daddy was never comfortable doing period films (the other one, *Under Capricorn,* was also unsuccessful). After this less-than-satisfying experience, it was with no regret that in March 1939, Alma, Hitch, Joan Harrison, and I boarded the *Queen Mary.* We were on our way to a new life and new film opportunities. America would be where the name Hitchcock would truly become legend.

CROSSING THE WATERS

"IT'S CRAZY OVER there," several of my parents' friends in Britain said. They were warning Hitch and Alma about America. According to them, not even Hitch would be able to keep his calm demeanor in Hollywood. They kept hearing: "Everything depends on maintaining your success," "You'll have to have a huge house," "If you don't move to a better one every few years, people will think you're slipping," and so on. My parents decided not to believe any of them. Perhaps their friends were just envious, but of course, aspects of what they were saying were true. Hollywood does have many pitfalls; we were just very careful not to fall in any of them. So despite the warnings, when we climbed onboard the *Queen Mary*, we did not look back. We were such a small, close family that we felt that as long as we had each other, we could weather almost anything. I was pretty much convinced we were never going to live in England again. On the ship, Alma and Hitch had a cabin and I shared mine with Joan Harrison who, I recall, was seasick during the entire trip. I don't think she ever even made it to the deck! I remember I'd come back to the cabin and I'd tell her what I had eaten for lunch or dinner, and she would become even sicker! To my parents' delight, I could sometimes be quite mischievous.

When we arrived in New York, the press was there to welcome us and I remember we had to take quite a lot of pictures on the ship. Daddy was already a celebrity in England, and David O. Selznick wanted to make sure that his arrival to the States was noticed and advertised across the United States. It was remarkable and quite a coup for Selznick to persuade Britain's number-one movie family to move to America—and of course he was responsible for it. Daddy was used to photographers, and both Mama and I never minded the press—in those days, they were less-intrusive than they are today. After we arrived in New York, Kay Brown, David O. Selznick's secretary, greeted us along with the press. We spent a weekend at her house in Amagansett, Long Island, with her husband, James Barrett, and their daughter, Laurinda. We then went to Florida to spend a few relaxing days in the sun. I think the British quite naturally gravitate to sunny weather. At least, Alma and I did. Hitch did not care so much. We went from New York to Chicago and took the Super Chief train, which brought us to Los Angeles. Our two dogs, Edward and Jenkins (Jenky), accompanied us. We also brought our two household maids, but one quit and went back home and the other quit, too, and became a chiropractor.

When we arrived in Los Angeles, Selznick set us up at the Wilshire Palm, a luxurious place complete with a tennis court and a pool—that's when I knew I loved America better than

England. The Ritz Brothers were our neighbors. I remember Franchot Tone, Joan Crawford's ex-husband, lived there, too. We were also thrilled to be reunited with our friend Charles Bennett, who now had a writing deal at Universal. Charles was one of the few British expatriates my parents liked to socialize with.

While my parents were adjusting to their new lifestyle, I also had my share of assimilating to the American way. I went to Marymount Catholic School for girls and was at first quite unhappy there. It seemed I had always been very unlucky with schools. The other kids laughed at me because I had a British accent, so I ended up being arrogant to all of them. Like my father, I eventually lost my accent—and made a few friends. One of them was a girl named Sheila who happened to be the daughter of filmmaker George Fitzmaurice, who had worked with Alma and Hitch back in England in the early twenties.

Small world. My mother pretty much kept her British accent all of her life. My teachers knew who my father was, but unless you were a regular filmgoer, the name Hitchcock did not resonate as much as it would in the years to come, so I never got special treatment because of who my parents were. And then, in Hollywood, the child of a celebrity was not that unusual. Alma took me to school every morning and picked me up in the afternoons. That was great quality time with Mama, and we would talk about our day, what I did in school, and what she did at home or at the studio with Daddy. Those bonding experiences left a very positive feeling inside me. In the first few months after we arrived, Hitch was working on *Rebecca,* and Alma would tell me who was being cast in the leading roles. We were both very excited about this new film. It was not only a great story, but it also seemed to have a near-epic scale, something that was out of the ordinary and challenging for Daddy.

THROUGH THE YEARS Hitch and Alma lived in America, they only had three different homes. They knew the Wilshire Palm was temporary. As we settled, my parents decided to rent a house that belonged to our friend Carole Lombard. It was a British Tudor–style home, located at 609 Saint Cloud Road. Carole's home was known as "The Farm," for no apparently better reason than that its style was simple. There were a few open beams, and the staircase led upstairs from the sitting room, into which one entered country-style—without the formality of first negotiating a front hall. "The Farm" was rich in fireplaces, a point of undoubted appeal to my parents particularly, who had the usual British love of an open log fire. The grounds were beautiful with trees and grass. It was a very peaceful place. For Alma and myself, there was a tennis court at the side of the house. Hitch could occasionally be coaxed to play, but having no love of strenuous exercise and a great love for music, he was much happier left to occupy himself with his collection of symphonic recordings.

Our house was entirely white inside as well as out when we moved in, and I remember the dining room floor was red tile. Alma and Hitch decided to have the paint changed throughout, the dining room walls paneled, the cold tile floor replaced with parquet, and in spite of having increased the size of the dining room, somehow they managed a very attractive little bar in an alcove off the sitting room. Daddy disliked Scotch, but he loved to have a gin and orange juice concoction of his own before dinner and had developed a taste for fine wines. Our dinner parties around that time were generally small and usually informal, but the food prepared by Alma always elicited rave reviews.

We had brought over some furniture from the cottage at Shamley Green and other pieces from our London flat. That helped give us a sense of our British history in our California home.

THOUGH NONE OF us golfed, my parents eventually bought a house on the fifteenth fairway of the Bel Air golf course. Mama and I were in charge of finding potential properties, and we looked for a long time. But Daddy had right of first refusal; he had been very specific on what he wanted—and what he didn't want. "What I want is a home," I recall him saying, "not a movie set with a heating plant added. All I need is a snug little house with a good kitchen, and the devil with a swimming pool. First thing the real estate agents start talking about is the pool. Then they discuss the tennis court. Finally they get around talking about the barbecue arrangements in back of the rose garden. They never talk about the house. Maybe they're ashamed of it."

Eventually, Alma and I found a place we liked and were anxious to show it to Daddy. He came to see it but seemed completely unimpressed. Then, on Alma's birthday, Daddy gave her a purse, and inside it was a little box. Inside the box was a golden key. It was the key to the house she and I had chosen. I still have that key. In the spring of 1942, our new address became 10957 Bellagio Road; my father had bought the house for $40,000—a great investment considering that they would live there for the rest of their life. Alma set out to create a home that would match the Hitchcocks' own family serenity. On the housekeeping side this meant that our home had to be as orderly and tidy as one of Hitch's film sets. That part was easy because Daddy was neat almost to the point of obsession. In his own words, he was an "ashtray emptier," and he never washed his hands without using two or three towels to wipe dry the basin and faucets.

In the sixties, my parents decided to enlarge the kitchen (Alma did all the cooking, with the help of a very kind woman named Chrystal) and added a walk-in refrigerator and a wine cellar. With two bedrooms and a den, no pool or tennis court, it was not a typical Hollywood house. My parents' bedroom offered a blend of modern, Chinese, and French décor. One might have expected my bedroom to be a youthful version of this same "understatement" in modern decoration. But I had a mind of my own. My room had bouffant organdy and taffeta, stuffed animals, doodads, and pictures of my favorite movie stars.

I just loved spending quiet weekends. I remember Hitch and Alma reading (she loved biographies of theater celebrities). Alma would put on one of her Broadway musical albums (she particularly liked Jerome Kern). Life at home was simple and cozy.

In the early forties, my parents bought a fairly large country house in Santa Cruz, two hours south of San Francisco. The property was 200 acres, set on top of a hill with a vineyard, and overlooked the Monterey Bay. My parents loved entertaining there almost better than they did in the city. Alma and I would often drive up there together on Thursdays—in those days, it took about nine hours. We would stop at the local inn in a small town called Santa Maria for lunch or take sandwiches and have a picnic. Daddy would then come and join us for the weekend the next day.

My parents loved art and became serious collectors after we moved to America. Our home had beautiful original paintings by artists such as Rodin, Utrillo, Paul Klee, Vlaminck, and others. Alma and Hitch decorated the house together. There were very few bits of film memorabilia except for production paintings done for *Lifeboat* (1944), which my parents displayed in the bar area. One of my favorite pieces was at the Santa Cruz house. It was a mosaic of birds based on a drawing by French artist Braque. Mama's own favorite was a painting of a street of Paris called "Rue des Abesses" by Utrillo. My parents collected two other oil paintings by the same artist.

Santa Cruz was a real escape for my parents, and many of their friends loved going there. Connie Erickson, wife of Doc Erickson, one of my father's colleagues, remembers: "My husband had been working with Mr. Hitchcock and one day, we got invited to spend the weekend with him and his wife up in

Santa Cruz. It was to be just the four of us. Alma and Hitch met us at the airport. We climbed in a huge car, Alma drove while Hitch chatted with us on our way to "The Ranch," as they called it. What a treat to arrive at this lovely home, nestled in the hills, so quiet and private with colorful hanging baskets of begonias everywhere. Only the English can do so well with their gardens and flowers—a built-in talent. Being so young at the time, I was a bit nervous, but once we got to the Hitchcock home, I felt at ease and we spent a couple of delightful days, eating (Alma cooked the meals, and Hitch chose the appropriate wine), and relaxing. Alma was the perfect hostess because she was simple and so understated. And Hitch was the same. My husband and I never felt we were at the Hitchcocks; we felt like we were in our own home.

"Years later, I flew to London with Pat for the Hitchcock hundredth birthday celebration. We took the train to Nottingham where Alma was born, and I simply loved discovering the neighborhood where she grew up. For some strange reason, Nottingham seemed familiar to me. It was then that I realized that Alma had recreated the beautiful feeling of the city

where she grew up in the house in Santa Cruz. Nottingham, I found out, is known as the flower city of England. Like in the Santa Cruz home, there were flowers everywhere. And no doubt, Alma was one of them."

AMERICA: THE FIRST DECADE
(1939-1949)

I READ A LOT as a child. I loved the *Nancy Drew* book
series. My parents had quite a library in London, and it
got even larger in the States. They had a complete collection of
famous trials, novels by Somerset Maugham, plays by William
Shakespeare, complete works of John Gallsworthy, John
Buchan, Charles Dickens, J. M. Barrie, and George Bernard
Shaw. The Shaw book collection is very special; the first volume
(*Immaturity*) was inscribed by the author to my mother as follows: "Of this edition, one thousand and twenty five copies
only have been printed, this is number 552 and is specially dedicated by the author to Alma Hitchcock (Alfred Hitchcock is her
husband). Signed: G. Bernard Shaw, 6 October, 1932."

But whether it was in England or in America, each time my father received a book or a script to consider as a potential project, he immediately gave it to my mother to read first. If she didn't like it, it was instantly rejected. If she liked it, she would pass it on to him. Interestingly, most of my father's films are based on existing material: novels, plays, short stories. Very few were original screenplays. Once a novel was acquired, many things changed during the adaptation to the screen, and my mother was very much part of that process early on. But her influence became even greater during my parents' first two decades in America. In the case of *Rebecca* (1940), the first American Hitchcock film, very little was changed from the novel by Daphne du Maurier. Although I think Daddy would have done a great film of the *Titanic* (the first film Selznick initially intended for him to direct), *Rebecca* was a perfect choice—Daddy had briefly considered buying the rights to the book when he was in England. It had the mysterious elements of some of his best British films while at the same time was a departure from any of his earlier pictures. For one thing, *Rebecca* was a *big* movie. Selznick, who was at the time completing *Gone With the Wind,* was of course brilliant at assembling the best creative teams, and he made sure that Daddy was surrounded with nothing but the best collaborators. Although my father declared on few occasions that, in retrospect, *Rebecca* was not a typical "Hitchcock" picture, he was able to emphasize, as customary, suspense, and add, as always, a little bit of humor.

Rebecca centers on the marriage of an innocent and naive young woman to a recently widowed aristocrat named Maxim de Winter. As the story unfolds, the "second Mrs. de Winter" (as in the novel; we never find out her given name) is confronted with the mysterious past of Maxim's first wife, Rebecca: Who was she? Was she good or evil? How was she killed? Was she murdered by Maxim, was it suicide, or was it an accident? In those days, it was up to the censors to decide *how* Rebecca really died. In the original book, Rebecca provokes Maxim, confronting him with tales of her infidelities, and he shoots her. Her death in the film version had to be completely accidental; Rebecca has discovered she has cancer. But when she provokes Maxim, she trips and takes a fatal fall. It's neither suicide nor murder (both big issues with censorship at the time)—*but* suicide was on her mind and murder on his.

During pre-production, the search for the actress to play the "second Mrs. de Winter" was almost as notorious as the search for Scarlett O'Hara in *Gone With the Wind*. When Laurence Olivier (who used to call me "Sausage"—believe me, it sounds a lot better when spoken in that delightful British accent of his) got the role of Maxim, Vivien Leigh, who was then married to him, auditioned for the part of the second Mrs. de Winter. Famous and nonfamous actresses auditioned for the part, and Hitch relied a lot on both Alma and Joan Harrison's opinions and would screen the tests with them. In a memo to David O. Selznick, Daddy reported Alma's and Joan's feedback on the screen tests that Anne Baxter and Margaret Sullavan were considered early on when Ronald Coleman was the contender for the role of the dashing Maxim de Winter.

Alma and Joan's opinion of Anne Baxter was that she was much more moving but feared that she would not be able to play love scenes due to her age and lack of experience.

Both Alma and Joan agreed that Sullavan was far ahead but should be made less sure of herself and characterized more as the girl in the book. Joan felt that Sullavan, if she got the part, would help relieve the monotony that might arise through the terrific number of scenes the leading lady had to play.

The opinion seemed to be that Anne Baxter would be definitely second choice after Margaret Sullavan. Another thing mentioned by both Alma and Joan in Baxter's favor was that her voice has a quality that could be taken easily for either English or American in the same manner as Ronald Colman's.

Alma was particularly concerned about how the role of the second Mrs. de Winter would be played. At first, she had to appear weak and somewhat victimized, but Alma felt that whomever got the role should not play coy or simpering to the point where she would become intolerable and irritating to the audience. It was important to feel sorry for her, while at the same time side with her. That was a balance only the actress playing the role could bring, and in the end, Joan Fontaine got the part. Joan brought the right blend of innocence and beauty to the role, and Daddy, following Alma's advice, made sure her performance stayed on the side of the audience.

The supporting cast was quite remarkable. Judith Anderson as the deranged and obsessive housekeeper Mrs. Danvers delivered a memorable performance. Her role was rather suggestive, and her obsession with preserving Rebecca's memory as if she were still alive offered an unnerving (and controversial) substance and subtext to the character given the time the film was made. George Sanders was Rebecca's "favorite cousin" Jack Favell; Nigel Bruce played Giles Lacey, Maxim's clumsy brother-in-law; Gladys Cooper was perfect as his wife, the condescending Beatrice Lacey; Florence Bates was a scene-stealer in the role of the cruel Mrs. Van Hopper, Joan Fontaine's employer at the beginning of the picture; and Leo G. Carroll, in his first of many appearances in my father's films, was perfect as the doctor who reveals Rebecca's secret at the end. This impressive cast proved that there was no such thing as a small role in a Hitchcock movie. They all served a purpose not only in terms of the plot but also added flavor to scenes that would have, played by the wrong actor, seemed mundane and forgettable.

Rebecca was a huge success and won an Oscar for Best Picture (it was Mr. Selznick, not Daddy, who got the statuette). I vividly remember the premiere in New York at Radio City Music Hall. Mama had a birthday dress I had as an infant reproduced for the occasion; I felt so special. I never tire of watching that film, and I know that both my father and mother were relieved that this first picture made in America was a complete success.

During filming, however, World War II was declared in England. Both Daddy and Mama were understandably in a panic, trying to reach their relatives back home. It was also a frustrating time for them because they wanted to contribute to the war efforts. Daddy was past the age of active enrollment in the army, but he immediately contacted his colleagues in the film industry in England and tried to find ways to help. There were two schools of thought. Producer Michael Balcon, for instance, denounced expatriates and accused them of deserting England. (Both Alma and Hitch were extremely hurt; Hitch was under contract and could not leave America.) Winston Churchill, on the other hand, tried to motivate British film-makers to fight back through their films. And that's how and why Daddy's next film, *Foreign Correspondent* (1940), evolved.

The film reunited my father with Charles Bennett, who co-wrote the script with Joan Harrison (they would both receive an Oscar nomination for their work on the film). *Foreign Correspondent* (formerly titled *Personal History*) was produced by Walter Wanger (with my father, as they used to say in the old studio days, "on-loan" from Selznick). It was a spy story with some amazing set pieces involving windmills (part of the film takes place in Holland), a plane crash in the ocean, and a complex love story (the hero falls in love with the daughter of a traitor). *Foreign Correspondent* was less a piece of propaganda as it had initially been intended, and yet, the film demonstrated that Hitch could deliver both an entertaining story but also have a message sprinkled throughout. The ending of the film was particularly chilling as the hero of the story, finding himself fully committed to fight Germany and the Nazi invasion, delivers a broadcast to America as the bombs are falling: "Keep those lights burning, cover them with steel, build them in with guns, build a canopy of battleships and bombing planes around them and, hello, America, hang on to your lights, they're the only lights left in the world." Two of the supporting roles were played by my parents' British colleagues: Herbert Marshall (*Murder!*) and Edmund Gwenn (*The Skin Game* and *Waltzes from Vienna*). George Sanders, who had just been in *Rebecca*, also joined the cast. Laraine Day was the female lead, and Joel McCrea played the title role. Robert Benchley had a small part and also wrote some of the witty dialogue for his part and others. One regret: My father had wanted Gary Cooper for the lead. Alma loved the idea as well, although I felt Joel McCrea was quite good in the role. The film was released in August 1940. America would enter the war some sixteen months later.

ALMA HAD GONE back to England and had brought her mother and her sister to America. Daddy had tried to do the same for his own mother, but she was stubborn and refused to leave. Yet London was not safe, so she did finally agree to move to Shamley Green. Daddy's brother moved nearby after he was bombed out of his London fish shop and kept a good eye on Grandma. From his trip to London, Daddy brought me back an empty incendiary bomb case, which I kept near my bed for many years.

GIVEN THE DEPRESSING times we lived in, I was only half-surprised when Alma told me that Daddy's next film had nothing to do with suspense; it was a screwball comedy titled *Mr. and Mrs. Smith* (1941). My parents were very close to Clark Gable and Carole Lombard. Daddy and Carole had wanted to work together and, with Alma's encouragement, they decided on *Mr. and Mrs. Smith*. The story: A couple (Lombard and Robert Montgomery) discovers that their marriage, through a technicality, is invalid. After provoking each other into the most hilarious situations,

they find out they can't live without each other and get back together. It is the least Hitchcockian of all of my father's American films, but at the same time, on the set, it was a match made in heaven for one very special reason—Lombard and Hitch had the same sense of humor and both enjoyed pulling pranks. At that point, my father was already famous for saying, "Actors are cattle" (which he often disputed: "I never said actors were cattle; what I said is that they should be treated like cattle!"). Carole took the quote literally, and on the first day of shooting, Daddy showed up on the set and saw three stalls, each containing a calf: They each had a tag around their necks with the names of the principal actors! Carole really had such a delightful personality, and when she died tragically a couple years later in a plane crash, my parents were so devastated. It was a huge loss not only because she was so young and such a gifted and beautiful actress, but because she was an extraordinary human being. My parents and I missed her very much, and I wish I had gotten to know her better—and longer.

I remember sitting with my parents in their home in Bel Air after some big celebrity had just passed away in the sixties. Somehow, Mama and I got on the subject of Carole Lombard and Clark Gable. Mama was telling me how devastating it was when Carole died in the plane crash. Shortly after Carole's death she and Daddy were on a train going somewhere and they found out that Clark Gable was also on the train. They sent him a note, asking if they could see him for a minute and he agreed. Alma was heartbroken when she saw his face; he was a changed man. Hitch and Alma cared very much for their friends. Because they had left England early on in their careers, they really felt that America had adopted them. Their American friends and colleagues were like family to them, and if anything happened to any one of them, they were deeply affected.

~

JUST LIKE IN England, it seemed my parents were always working on a film, even when the cameras were not rolling. Alma was always reading, writing, and rewriting. Hitch was always planning the next film, throwing ideas at Alma for her approval and insight. And their collaboration continued to flourish on their next film, *Suspicion* (1941). It was an important film, because it was the first of several Hitchcock films to star Cary Grant—a classic handsome leading man who instantly became a regular at our house. The film also starred some Hitchcock "regulars": Joan Fontaine (who would win an Oscar for her role in *Suspicion*), Dame May Whitty (*The Lady Vanishes*), and Nigel Bruce and Leo G. Carroll (both had starred in *Rebecca*). Auriol Lee, who portrayed Isobel Sedbusk, an Agatha Christie–type mystery writer, was also marvelous in the film and would play a major part that year in getting me my first role on Broadway.

The film was based on the novel *Before the Fact* and the screen adaptation was signed by three screenwriters: Samson Raphaelson, Joan Harrison, and Mama. Today, the film is a classic, but at the time, it put both my parents to the test—literally.

"I'm not too pleased about the way *Suspicion* ends," my father said on many occasions, and my mother definitely agreed with him. The book focused on a woman who gradually realizes that her husband is a murderer and who, out of love for him, allows herself to be killed by him. In the film adaptation, the woman, Lina McLaidlaw (Joan Fontaine), suspects her husband, Johnnie Aysgarth (Cary Grant), of planning her murder after discovering that he is a gambler and might have killed his best friend, Beaky (Nigel Bruce), for money. One night, Johnnie brings his wife a glass of milk (to make the milk really stand out, Daddy placed a lightbulb inside the glass!) and Lina thinks he's trying to poison her. In a final confrontation, Lina discovers that she was wrong all along. Johnnie still thinks they should break up, but in the end, Lina is able to convince him otherwise.

One idea that was discussed but never put on paper was quite interesting. It had Cary Grant's character bring the glass of poisoned milk to his wife who, knowing her fate, asks her husband to send a letter she has written to her mother in which she reveals that he is a killer. She drinks the milk and dies, and the film ends with the husband whistling his way to the mailbox. That idea was never realized. One reason was that the audience did not want to see Cary Grant as a killer. There remained the question of how to end the film. As soon as my parents read the book, they knew the ending with the wife letting the husband poison her would have to be changed.

Different possible endings were written.

Hitch and Alma took the film for a preview at the United Artists Theater in Pasadena, California, on June 13, 1941. The cards asked the following questions:

How did you like the picture? Excellent, Good, Fair, Poor.

Was the action in the picture entirely clear? If not, where was it confusing?

Was the dialogue entirely clear?

Did any parts seem too long? If so, what parts?

Did you like the ending?

Have you any other suggestions?

~

ALMA AND HITCH waited with great anxiety to read the cards and, for a moment, were reminded of their difficult time in England with *The Lodger*. A total of eighty cards were filled out. Most of the viewers felt the film was either excellent or good, with only few exceptions—among the most insulting comments: "Absolutely a waste of time to see anything with so low ideals" and "Junk the picture. Get a good cowboy story." I can only imagine my parents' faces when they read those lines. Daddy didn't care about the critics—Mama, either. But both cared about what the audience had to say, and some of the negative reactions they received on *Suspicion*—and other films—must have been difficult.

Ten days after this initial screening, another one took place at the Academy Theater in Inglewood. The film generally received positive feedback, but when rating the ending specifically, seventy-nine members of the audience liked it, fifty-four didn't, and eleven did not answer. Fifty-four was too large a number to dismiss. The final ending was completed and delivered on July 18, 1941: Lina never drinks the milk, and Lina and Johnnie have it out—she apologizes for suspecting him, he apologizes for being irresponsible. He never killed anyone, never even thought of it. Love prevails. The end.

Suspicion was generally well received, but some critics did pick up on the weak ending: "Hitchcock does a super job in creating and sustaining an enormously absorbing mood," Rose

Pelswick of the New York *Journal-American* wrote in her review. "Up until, that is, the last few minutes when, for some reason or other, tacked on an unconvincingly contrived happy ending." Logically, my parents were relieved when the movie did well at the box office, but they always remained dissatisfied with the way the film ended. It is nice to know that both Hitch and Alma were very humble; they never felt as if they knew it all or that they were always right. They knew when something worked and accepted when something did not. They had great honesty about their work and were their own toughest critics. *Suspicion* remains a good example of my parents' close collaboration.

Suspicion marked the first film that Hitch would do with Cary Grant. We all simply adored him. "One story Alma kept quoting," my daughter Mary remembers, "took place in the sixties. Cary Grant was a huge baseball fan and one day, took Alma and Hitch to a Dodger game. They sat in field-level seats and Cary explained the game to Alma. Alma would chuckle as she told the story: 'He was so handsome and so charming, I barely listened to what he was saying!' Eventually, Alma did listen and was surprised to hear that the pitcher's mount was actually raised!"

I ALWAYS WANTED to be an actress. When I was in boarding school in England, I acted in a number of plays. I was never intimidated by being on stage and never experienced stage fright. I remember my parents coming to see me perform in school. The first play I was in was called *The Little King Who Wouldn't Grow Up.* I played the little king. I was also the lead in *Rumpelstilskin.* When I told my parents I wanted to be an actress, they both simply said, "If you want to be an actress, you have to learn your craft." From then on, it was completely up to me. I was extremely determined (a trait I inherited from both Alma and Hitch). Rather than asking them if they approved, I think I was merely informing them of my choice to become an

actress. I was very independent in this respect, and as an only child both my parents gave me the right to be independent. My first "real" play, *Solitaire*, was in 1942, right after Pearl Harbor; it lasted only three weeks. I was eleven and Auriol Lee, who I had met on *Suspicion*, was set to direct six plays by John Van Druten, and *Solitaire* was one of them. Auriol wanted me to read for it, but she had to ask my parents first. They said, "Fine, just as long as she doesn't know what she is reading for." They didn't want me to be disappointed if I didn't get the part. John Van Druten, the playwright, came over one day, pretending that he needed to make some cuts in the dialogue and wanted somebody of the character's age to read the lines for him. So of course I believed him . . . and I got the part. It was a very exciting time—*Life* magazine even came and took pictures of my parents and me. In one of them, Daddy is giving me a watch as a congratulatory gift. (The play was such a flop, though, that the pictures never ran.)

Auriol Lee finished *Suspicion* and went back to New York on a cross-country auto trip and was killed tragically in a crash outside Kansas City on July 2, 1941. I remember hearing the news; I couldn't believe it. Sudden death was a difficult concept for me to grasp at such a young age. My parents and I, along with everyone else who had just finished working with her on the film, were devastated.

A director named Dudley Digges replaced Auriol as director of *Solitaire.* The play opened at the Plymouth Theater. Daddy was already shooting his next film, *Saboteur* (1944), and couldn't make it. I played a young girl named Virginia Stewart who befriends an old hobo living in an arroyo near her home out west. My stage father was played by Ben Smith, who had started the theatrical fad of growing beards to save razor blades for the war. I had also made a contribution and, along with my friend Ann French, the daughter of an actor producer named Harold French, had proudly knitted squares for British War Relief Blankets. Ann's mother had been killed in an air raid.

Alma was there with me the whole time, as my guardian and as my greatest fan. The play was most certainly a complete disaster, but I didn't care. I got some amazing reviews—one of them said I was "a promising talent." I was very happy with my work and was extremely comfortable on stage. It was known at the time as the longest child's role in theatrical history. I appeared in every one of the ten scenes. I was becoming a mini-celebrity and was interviewed by the *New York Post*. The purpose of the article was to prove that I had been misquoted in a column and had referred to Daddy as "my old man." I had apparently said, "I'm not afraid of the part [in *Solitaire*], the director, the audience, or anything else, just as long as my old man doesn't come to see. He'd frighten me to death." I had never said such a thing. Alma was a bit upset. The *New York Post* article was to set the record straight. Reading over it, it mentioned things I had forgotten: Back home I had two turtles, and I told the reporter I wanted to own a total of twenty-six, one for each letter of the alphabet. I said I would have their names printed on the turtles' shells. I had already come up with some funny names: "Eggellbert," "Gussie," and "Quincey."

On opening night, January 27, 1942, I received many telegrams from family members, friends, and colleagues of my parents. Charles Bennett, Robert Benchley, David O. Selznick, May Whitty (*The Lady Vanishes*), and Judith Anderson (*Rebecca*) were among those sending me their warmest wishes and congratulations. It was very special to be acknowledged by people I admired, and by such professionals. It gave me great confidence and made me feel like I was being taken seriously by my peers.

~

WHILE ALMA AND I were in New York for *Solitaire*, Daddy was doing *Saboteur*, which, in my eyes, was an unofficial American remake and adaptation of *The 39 Steps*. A man (Robert Cummings) is wrongly accused of a murder and sabotage and has to travel cross-country looking for the real criminals to claim his innocence. In the process, he not only defeats a group of traitors, but he also falls in love. Daddy came up with the frame of the story; Alma was very enthusiastic about it and Hitch gave it to Selznick who, in turn, hired John Houseman (co-founder, with Orson Welles, of the Mercury Theater and by the time *Saboteur* came along, a producer with Selznick) to supervise a first draft of the script by Peter Viertel. Joan Harrison also did some writing but had to leave to become a producer on her own project, *Phantom Lady*. Dorothy Parker did a final rewrite, adding a lot of humor and bringing more depth to the characters. But Selznick did not want to produce the film. He tried selling it to RKO and Fox and both turned it down. It was eventually bought by producers Frank Lloyd and Jack Skirball for Universal Pictures. For the leads, Daddy wanted (as with *Foreign Correspondent*) Gary Cooper and Barbara Stanwick, but they both passed. Bob Cummings and Priscilla Lane then came on board.

There were two types of villains in the story; the classy, charming, and elegant traitor played by Otto Kruger, and the actual killer portrayed by Norman Lloyd, who was to become a very close collaborator and friend of my parents. I thought Bob Cummings was perfect in the role of the wrong man accused of murder; he would work with Daddy a few years later on *Dial M for Murder* (1954). We didn't socialize with him much at the time we were doing *Saboteur,* but later on, he would have extravagant birthday parties for his kids and would invite my husband and I and our daughters. "Mom would walk us to the door and leave," my daughter Mary recalled. "I always thought it was strange that Bob rarely came down. His wife would take us upstairs to his room to see him."

When Bob started his own television show, *The Bob Cummings Show,* I was supposed to test for the part Ann B. Davis played; I had to turn it down because I became pregnant.

~⁀

ONE OF THE most amazing moments in *Saboteur* was the final confrontation between Bob Cummings and Norman Lloyd on top of the Statue of Liberty. The sequence was carefully plotted and storyboarded—the villain ends up hanging on top of the statue while trying to escape; Bob reaches out to him and grabs his sleeve. It unravels, and Norman takes a spectacular fall. The visual effects in that sequence were groundbreaking and orchestrated by art director Robert Boyle (who would work on several other films with Daddy). You really got the illusion that Norman Lloyd was falling from the top of the Statue of Liberty. It was breathtaking and even if *Saboteur* was somewhat

Mama and Bob Cummings enjoying a restful afternoon at Santa Cruz.

perceived as a B action movie, that sequence alone elevated it to vintage Hitchcock.

Although Mama was not as involved with *Saboteur* as she had been on *Suspicion,* Norman Lloyd had a chance to get to know her during the production and their friendship and collaboration grew from there: "Whenever I think of Alma, I think of her smiling. Behind the glasses were those merry eyes that could become mischievous with the proper provocation. She had the gift of making you feel most welcome. One felt it was her approval that admitted you to the Hitchcock household. Of course, Hitch himself would have needed to give his assent. One always felt Alma's presence. Her importance to Hitch was inestimable. She was firm in her opinions of material, and her voice could take on a steely ring if she was displeased. There was something about the way she stood, her legs planted firmly, that gave forth a sense of strength.

Mama with Peggy and Norman Lloyd having afternoon tea in the garden.

"And then there was her sense of fun. There were times in the first years I knew Hitch that I would attempt some practical joke that might be not unlike the practical joking for which, at one time, he had been well known. When, at my suggestion, I proposed to Alma I pose as a policeman with a fellow actor, both of us in uniform and disguise, and accost Hitch at the airport in Los Angeles, she did not discourage us. But at the last moment our courage failed, and we never went through with the plan.

"However, there was a time in New York when the Hitchcocks were staying at the Saint Regis Hotel and were about to leave for the airport to fly back to Los Angeles. On the way to the hotel to say good-bye to them, I had a brainstorm. I stopped off at Walgreens drugstore where the Broadway actors bought their makeup and purchased a stick of Stein's black face and a small hand mirror. It was my intention to present myself to Alma and Hitch as a reporter from the Harlem newspaper. To that end, I bought a copy of the *Amsterdam News,* a Harlem daily. I made my way over to the Saint Regis, got off the elevator on the four-teenth floor, where I proceeded to apply the black face to my skin and, covering my abundant red hair with a hat pulled far down on my head, I rang the bell of the suite. Alma opened the door. I immediately revealed in a whisper while taking off my hat who I was. Alma welcomed me in with a great laugh and said that Hitch was down in the King Cole Bar finishing an interview and would be coming back to the suite shortly. She then entered the conspiracy. She would call down to the bar and inform Hitch it was time to leave for the airport. When he rang the bell of the suite, it was she who planned that I open the door in full make-up. We were eager to see Hitch's reaction to this unknown per-son in his suite. She called down to the bar, and in a few minutes, Hitch rang the bell. Alma stepped out of sight but stayed at a van-tage point where she could see Hitch. I tugged my hat down as far as I could and opened the door. Hitch stared at me for a long beat and then said, 'We'll be late for the plane, Norman.' Alma and I could never quite pin down Hitch's reaction in that long beat before he revealed my identity, but we enjoyed the prank.

"We were in Washington for the premiere of *Saboteur.* Drew Pearson was host, Maxim Litvinoff (the war was still on) was guest speaker, black tie, cocktails before dinner, etc. . . . Clearly, it was a very important occasion of some diplomatic impor-tance and a great setting for the opening of the picture. Alma, my wife Peggy, Jack Skirball (the producer of the picture), and I were present at the cocktail party, but there was no sign of Hitch. Alma became concerned. She suggested I go up to their suite and check on Hitch. I proceeded to do so. He was in a state. The zipper of the trousers to his dinner jacket had become stuck. There he was, trying unsuccessfully to get it unstuck. I stood by helplessly. Finally, he had the solution. 'Get Alma,' he said in desperation. A good idea, I thought. I turned and went back to the party. I sought out Alma and described the situation to her. Smiling, she left the party and not long after, returned with Hitch. Another example of Hitch's dependency on her."

~

"MAMA," I ONCE asked Alma casually, "which one is your favorite of Daddy's films?" Without hesitating one bit, she replied, *Shadow of a Doubt*. It was Hitch's favorite, too. Mine is *Notorious* (1946). *Shadow of a Doubt* (1939) centers around the perfect American family: the Newtons. Perfect, that is, until the mother's brother, Uncle Charlie, comes and stays with them. The older daughter, named Charlie after her uncle, admires him but slowly starts suspecting that he might be the notorious "merry widow murderer." She eventually discovers that her uncle is indeed a monster, who will stop at nothing to get away with murder. Their final confrontation on a train turns deadly as Uncle Charlie struggles with his niece; she fights back, and he trips and falls under the wheel of an oncoming train. The film was a complete success, beginning with the script. The original idea was brought to my father by a writer named Gordon McDonell (his wife, Margaret, worked for Selznick). Both my parents were immediately seduced by the concept of the uncle symbolizing menace coming to a small town. Writer Thornton Wilder (famous at that time for his play *Our Town*) was brought in to work on the script. Wilder and Daddy traveled together to Santa Rosa, California, where the story was set, to find locations for the film and to incorporate the spirit of that small town into the script. Thornton had to leave for the army, and another playwright, Sally Benson, took over (she had just written a hit play titled *Junior Miss*). Alma co-wrote the script as well—that film was probably her proudest achievement. The Newton family was just brilliantly conceived: There is the father (Henry Travers), a man who likes to read murder mysteries and who constantly jokes about killing the next-door neighbor, played by Hume Cronyn in his first screen role. The mother, Emma, was played by Patricia Collinge, who brought warmth, heart, and humor to the character. The two young kids were played by Edna May Wonacott and Charles Bates. Charlie, the older daughter, was played by Teresa Wright, and the evil Uncle Charlie, Joseph Cotten (I admit I had a huge crush on him).

The making of the film was a family affair. We all went up to Santa Rosa for the shoot and all worked hard (Hitch was directing, Alma writing, and I was helping Edna May Wonacott rehearse her lines and coaching her). As I said, Daddy was notorious for insisting on shooting his films on soundstages; he did not like going on location, but in this case, he and Alma enjoyed being in that small town. I remember when Hitch and Thornton Wilder had found this wonderful little old house that matched exactly what Daddy wanted for the Newton home. They made a deal, but when we went up to start filming, the owners were so excited that they had completely repainted the house—and so we had to have it dirtied down!

The film was about a family, and there was definitely a family spirit on the set; we all played games together between takes, had dinners, and threw parties all through filming. I recall we all went to a Chinese restaurant in San Francisco one evening, and some lady (who might have been the owner) passed around the table this hundred-year-old egg while Joseph Cotten kept making jokes about it. It was hard not to laugh as the poor lady was trying to give us a lecture about the egg.

But happiness was not to last; my father's mother, Emma, had been very ill and finally passed away on September 26. It was a very sad time for all of us, especially for Daddy, who wished he could have been near her. While Emma Newton, the mother in *Shadow of a Doubt,* was not based on my grandmother, even though they have the same name, I can't help but think a bit about Grandma whenever I watch the film. Her kindness, her beauty, her simplicity, and her humor are all very memorable. A few months after Emma passed away, William, Daddy's brother, died of heart failure in his home. We stuck together during this very difficult time.

~

ALMA ALWAYS ENCOURAGED Hitch to do new things. Like him, she felt that the only way to grow as a filmmaker was to take chances while always keeping the audience in mind. And *Lifeboat* (1944), Daddy's next picture, was indeed an interesting experiment. It almost completely took place aboard a lifeboat, with just a few survivors from a ship wrecked by a German submarine. The story was written by *the* John Steinbeck, and the screenplay was by Jo Swerling. It was a perfect opportunity to put under a magnifying glass a small group of people from different social groups as they relate not only to each other during a time of war, but also toward a German they rescue from the water. The film was extremely well cast: Hume Cronyn, John Hodiak, William Bendix, and the incredible Tallulah Bankhead to name a few. I'll never forget the time Hitch told Alma and I the most hilarious story about Ms. Bankhead. It appeared she did not wear panties and, therefore, would offer a generous view of her—let's say—person, each time she climbed inside the lifeboat to do a scene. It got back to the front office and, Daddy received a memo asking him to tell Ms. Bankhead to dress properly. Daddy looked at the memo and simply said, "I don't like to get involved with departmental disputes. I mean, I can't tell if this is the responsibility of wardrobe, makeup, or the hair dressing department!" Listening to Daddy telling that story kept Alma and I laughing for weeks—and nobody ever talked to Ms. Bankhead about her dress code.

One of the great dilemmas on the film was to figure out how and where Daddy was going to make his cameo appearance. With the film taking place in a lifeboat, it was hard to come up with something practical. Daddy would sit at the dinner table

and try to solve this with Mama—he even suggested playing a corpse, floating by at the beginning of the film. But at the time, Daddy was on a diet, "painfully working my way from three hundred pounds to two hundred pounds," as he once admitted. And so he decided to pose for a fake newspaper ad, showing "before and after" results for an imaginary diet product called Reduco. The audience could see the ad when actor William Bendix opened an old newspaper (in fact, a prop created for the film). To his surprise, after the film came out, Daddy was submerged with letters from overweight people inquiring about Reduco!

After shooting was completed, Daddy's friend back in England, producer Sidney Bernstein, asked him to come and do two short propaganda films for the British Ministry of Information. Sidney Bernstein was with the head of the film division of the Ministry of Information during the war, and he was thrilled when Daddy accepted to do the films (which were titled *Aventures Malgache* and *Bon Voyage*). Both films were tributes to the French Resistance (they were done with the technical help of the Free France forces) and were shown in parts of

France where Germany was losing power in order to inform on the important role of the resistance. Daddy was very proud of having done those pictures, as it was his way of contributing to war efforts. Hitch made other contributions to propaganda films and would direct Jennifer Jones in a "Buy War Bonds" short in 1943 produced by David O. Selznick. But his absence had left Mama on her own to deal with the editing of *Lifeboat.* Daryl F. Zanuck, the head of 20th Century Fox (the studio producing the picture), wanted to have *Lifeboat* recut. Alma became very frustrated with the situation because she didn't like to deal with the politics of the studio. She felt caught between the demands of the studio and trying to remain true to Hitch's vision. I recall she nearly had a nervous breakdown over it. In the end, she felt only Hitch could deal with this, and she begged him to rush back home after he was done with the French films—and he did.

While Hitch was helping war efforts, Alma was also concerned about making a contribution or at least a statement; she planted a victory garden, and she was an air raid warden in Bel Air. One day, I was home from school and the neighborhood had organized a drill. When the siren went off, Mama put on her hat and we ran a couple blocks down the street. No one else came . . . at least, not for a while. Finally, when people showed up, everyone wondered, "What do we do next?" We decided someone had to pretend to be injured, so I played the victim. It was much-needed comic relief during a time when there was none, when the whole absurdity and cruelty of war was always on our minds.

~

DESPITE THE FAILURE of my first play, I continued to hope for other roles, and *Violet* by Whitfield Cook was an opportunity I didn't want to miss. Whitfield remembers, "I got to know Pat and Alma through my play *Violet;* it was about a thirteen-year-old

girl who was a bit of a brat, and it was a lot of fun. It was almost farcical. Pat had done one play in New York, *Solitaire* about a young girl and a tramp. The way we thought of Pat for the lead in *Violet* was one day, I was on a train with a publicist, Albert Margulies, who worked a lot with Hitch. He read the script and liked it and passed it on to the Hitchcocks. They loved it and of course, Pat was dying to do it. So that's how it started, that's how I met the family. From then on, we became great friends. For about ten years, we socialized and worked together, and the Hitchcocks were my best friends. Before I met the family, I didn't know much about Alma but I had always heard that Hitch respected her opinion enormously. I don't want to imply that she was necessarily the power behind the throne, but her opinion was very important to Hitch. As far as I can remember—at least when I was working with them—she was not always on the set but she went to the dailies about every other day and would give her opinion to Hitch.

"Albert Margulies, who introduced me to the Hitchcocks, produced *Violet;* he raised all the money. *Violet* was based on nineteen stories I had written in a popular magazine called *Redbook* over a period of four or five years. At that time I was under contract to MGM, and they had been interested in buying those stories—but because I was under salary already, I was going to make no money, so I told them no thank you. When the play got underway, MGM became interested again and made a new offer. I accepted. I think the amount I received was the highest ever paid to an author for an unproduced play. But that meant that MGM had to buy out Al Margulies and they had to finance the entire stage production.

"Looking back, I remember meeting Pat, Hitch, and Alma for the first time at the exact same time. I went to the house, and the first thing I realized was that they were all real people— no Hollywood stuff, very real, and very, very nice. Pat was very anxious to play the role, and we didn't really do an audition. Once we met, she had the part. We did have a reading in Los Angeles, but that was it. She had a lovely sense of comedy, and we couldn't think of anyone else who could have played this part. She was extremely good in it—and she was very funny. My God, she worked so hard. We all worked hard.

"Hitch was a wonderful man—a very good storyteller. He loved talking about what his next picture was going to be. He was amazing at conveying what he was going to do. Of course, he was already testing his ideas on you.

"Pat and Alma came to New York for the rehearsals. We were going to open at the Belasco Theater, and it was empty at the time so we were able to rehearse there as well—that's not always the case. The nice thing was that I immediately got the sense that both Hitch and Alma were extremely supportive of Pat. Pat would star in two of the films I wrote for Hitch: *Stage*

Fright in a small but memorable part and *Strangers on a Train* in a much bigger role—and she was wonderful in both films. I also remember liking her very much in *Psycho;* hers wasn't a big role, but you couldn't forget her.

"Pat, Alma, and I had a great relationship during the rehearsals and would go out at night, have dinners, and socialize. We rehearsed it and opened in New Haven and Boston—and it went very well. If we had kept it out of New York, we would have been fine, but the second we got to the city, it was a complete disaster. But at least I had made new friends in Hitch, Alma, and Pat.

"I knew the play was a flop on opening night in New York. As I said, it had gone wonderfully in New Haven and Boston—people were laughing exactly where they should be laughing. But in New York, half the laughs never came. I don't know why. I seem to recall I got out of the theater three-quarters of the way through the performance and went across the street to a bar. But Alma stayed. And of course, I had to go back to talk to the cast when the show was over, and Alma was extremely worried—not for Pat, but for me. Pat was disappointed but very confident, and the attacks were directed at the material, not at the performances. But I was fine with the situation, although I must say that Alma's concerns for me proved that she was a good friend and only worried of my well-being, not of the box-office receipts. Alma, Hitch, Pat, and I stayed great friends despite the fact that the play was a disaster, and when Alma became an American citizen in 1950, I was her witness. We went all the way to downtown Los Angeles, which was dreary even in those days, and she took the oath with many other people. Then we went to a nice lunch, and that was the celebration. Hitch would become an American citizen five years later, in 1955. Many other social and professional occasions would follow—including having the Hitchcocks as my witnesses at my wedding!"

~~)

ALMA DID NOT write a lot of letters. She did not keep a diary, either. So I was surprised and pleased when I found a few letters Alma sent to Carol Stevens, Daddy's super secretary, that chronicle our time in New York for *Violet*. Some names I could not identify but decided to show the letters unedited.

September 21, 1944

> From the Wyndham Hotel,
> 42 West 58th Street, New York

Dear Carol:

Many thanks for your long letter. I'm really trying to keep all the expenses down. It's too bad we were here two weeks before the rehearsals started, and also that she [Pat] is not being paid for rehearsals. I think we shouldn't have moved from Hollywood until the contract was signed, but we'll know another time. Actually it's not too bad here. I mean the rooms. The weather hasn't helped much—very dreary and humid. I'll answer your questions first. [Our dog] Edward doesn't miss [our other dog] Johnnie at all. In fact, I think he prefers being alone, sleeps most of the time. Whit Cook seems to be getting along very well so far with the direction. Up to today, they've only been sitting and reading, but I believe they'll get on the stage today and when they begin to move around, it will be easier to judge. He seems to know what he wants. The model for the set looks good. The cast is good; I don't think they'll mean much to you, but the principals are all well known here. Harvey Stevens is Pete, Helen Claire, Lili, Paula Trueman, Aunt Esther, Dore Meranda, Elfie. The kids seem pretty good and natural. Whit has done quite a bit of polishing on the script. The dates are as follows: New Haven opening: October 12th, Boston October 16th.

It all depends how it goes whether it's one or two weeks in Boston, and that affects the opening here. It's set for the Belasco Theater; they're rehearsing there already. Nice theater, too. Pat is getting a good break with publicity. I've sent Mr. H [Daddy] some proofs of pictures. I think the character looks quite good. That's about all the news on the play to date. Last night we went to see *Frenchman's Creek* [based on a novel by Daphne du Maurier]. I didn't like it. Pat did. The audience laughed at the wigs and clothes of [Actor Basil] Rathbone and [Ralph] Forbes— Joan [Fontaine] looks lovely and that's about all. We saw her afterward; she must be back on the coast now. I liked the Gary Cooper picture [it could have been: *The Story of Dr. Wassell, Saratoga Trunk,* or *Casanova Brown,* all three released that year]. Very slight but a good setup. We saw the Jean Arthur one the other day [*The Impatient Year*]. I thought it was a bore. I don't think Lee Bowman is nearly strong enough to carry the part. I left this letter yesterday. The doctor for the insurance has just been here—apparently I'm sound in mind and limb, so Mr. H will have to push me off the top of the Empire State to get rid of me. I hope you can read this appalling writing. When Mr. H comes, get him to bring my typewriter, will you. I just can't write at all. I miss the house and garden so much— and Mr. H. I don't think I can do this again. Anyway, Pat manages very well. Must finish now and go to the theater. PM are going with us to do a story on Pat and Brooklyn! Love to you and Adele. When you speak to her, I'd love to hear from her confidentially when she has a minute, how the Allen picture is going. Did Mr. H tell you about Bob Stevenson, Frances [director friend and his future wife]— rather sweet. Love again from us both.

Alma H.

~~⌇~~

[not dated]
My dear Carol,

We are getting along alright. Things are dreadfully expensive here, much higher than LA, especially food. I had to pay the month's bill in advance here. So here's the receipt. The apartment is not as nice as the other one, but I think we're lucky getting it—at this price, too. They are very short of help here—and as a result everything looks neglected—but with a little diplomacy, I'm getting it a little better. Got the housekeeper to change a chair that was very dirty and now have a nice clean one! You'll have heard all the news of the play from Mr. H I'm sure—of my little disagreement with Mr. Haning over the terms of the contract (he's the H to ring my sister and see if she has any red paints she can let him have). I'll write you again soon, when there is any more news to report.

Love from Pat and I, Yours, Alma H.

~~⌇~~

October 7, 1944
Dear Carol,

Here's a few more bills and a list of the stubs on my checkbook—if the play doesn't run a few months we'll be well out, I should say. Pat is working like a slave, literally never has a minute. She seems to be keeping well. She had a pain in her left side one day, so I had her checked up by Al's doctor, but it only proved to be a little muscular trouble (that's what the doctor's check is for). I've paid up another month in advance here. The new management have taken over and are beginning to clean up a bit. I was very alarmed when I heard someone has been breaking in the house. I told Mr. H to inform the Bel-Air people, they'll put an extra watcher on I'm sure. Probably Chrystal's been talking too much about me being away. I'll have to write you later about the play. I really can't tell at this stage how it's going. One day it looks hopeful, next day looks lousy. We'll know better after an audience has seen it. We've had the strangest weather. It turned real windy, everyone wore fur coats, now it's warm again and quite summery. What a nerve Chrystal wanting to take her husband up to Santa Cruz. Anyway, isn't she going to look after our house while Mr. H is away or is the idea to close it up eventually? I must close now, have to go and meet Pat.

Love, Alma Hitchcock.

～ↄ

10/29/1944 (Sunday)
My dear Carol:

Oh, what a dreary week. You will have heard, I'm sure, about the *dreadful* notices *Violet* got. I've never read such a bunch. I sent them on to [Producer] Jack Skirball, so you'll see those. They tried to be kind to Pat with one exception. They certainly crucified Whit Cook. Pat has taken it all splendidly. Her only concern is for Whit. I nearly cried on the second night. My views on actors has changed considerably. They all put on such an act of gaiety and went on the stage giving better performances than they'd ever given. Actually, all the audiences since the first night seem to like it. But I don't think they can possibly survive. They have to keep it on three weeks, so unless a miracle happens next week, off it will come. I haven't decided yet what our plans will be. I don't think it's fair to bring Pat back immediately so we might stay until Mr. H comes back. Maybe something else will turn up. I'm afraid we'll be well out of pocket—but I guess we'll have to mark it down as part of Pat's training. She certainly has learned a lot from it that will be most valuable to her in the future. By the way, [Samuel] Raphaelson's play, which opened two nights after us, also had pretty bad notices, but I think he'll pull through with the advance bookings they have. It's all very interesting and definitely not the business to invest one's money in! I rather pain for California, really miss it this time. I hope you had a good time on your short vacation. We're staying in bed today, having dinner with Kate Blumberg tonight.

Lots of love, Alma H.

November 10, 1944
My dear Carol,

It was nice talking to you yesterday on the phone. I don't think there is anything else on the painting I can think of just now. There is one little thing Zehnder might do while he's there—you know the swing door between the dining room and the kitchen—I think it might be easier if he could put one of those springs on that will enable it to be left open if needed—we had those at the old house, and when the table is being laid, etc. it saves a lot of the wearing of the paintwork. Maybe these are not obtainable now. Oh, and one other thing—ask him to check up where the tiles join the edge of the sink in the kitchen. Water sometimes drips through onto the drawer underneath—I think there is some porcelain preparation that can be put along—it was especially on the lefthand side. Mr. Rosenback gave me the enclosed bill again—I think I did send it to you—it was for the mounting of my sapphire. I think the photos were very good. Did I tell you I was at Bob Stevenson's wedding? I knew they were coming out and said they could go up to Santa Cruz for their honeymoon, but didn't hear any more about it, so obviously, they decided not to. I had a letter from Joan, she says [our dog] Johnnie is very well behaved. Since talking to you I've been wondering whether perhaps I should send [our other dog] Edward after all, for it's going to be even worse getting him used to the St. Regis when we move over. So I'll get on to a kennel here and see what I can do, and will let you know. I had to leave off this letter the other day. On Sunday we sent out to spend the day with Mr. and Mrs. Murray Silverstone at Scarsdale, had quite a nice day, but it was dreadfully cold. I've made the reservations at the St. Regis for us from December 1st. They were very nice and obliging about it—they have a new rule there now, all bookings have to go through one particular man. The day I went to see him he said he'd let me know during the week, but instead he called me up the same afternoon and said it was all fixed. At the moment we are living on the rest of Pat's salary—I will let you know when that is exhausted. I'm hoping it will last until we go over to the St. Regis.

Here is the list of checks I've drawn on my account to date—on the new checkbook:

$31, Oct. 28, Dr. Sterling (board for Edward)
$25, Oct. 31, cash (b-day present to Grandma)
$36.89, Oct. 31, Wyndham (odd expenses)
$7.58, Nov. 8, St. Regis Flowers (for Leonard Lyon's wife and baby)
$20, Nov. 9, Acme radio (rental)
$19.40, Nov. 11, Hamilton House (theater tickets)

I sent you my old stubs, didn't I? By the way, my mother had an accident to her false teeth plate and has to have something done to it which will cost $50—I wrote and told her to use the $25 I sent her for her birthday, and perhaps you would call Eva [Alma's sister] and see if they need the other $25—I doubt whether they will have that amount to spare. Would you mind? Well I don't think there is any more startling news. I don't like the sound of these new V2 things over England. I do hope Mr. H gets back as soon as he can. Love and thanks for your lovely long letter. Pat sends her love to you, too, maybe she'll get down to writing you now.

Yours, Alma Hitchcock.

PS: Would you mind asking Chrystal to send on my two woolen vests—also it might be a good idea to tell Jo, the gardener, to plant the tulip bulbs I had in last year—they are in the cupboard with the gardening tools—put them in front of the roses—and I think he might add some more to them. I certainly agree we'll make a change when I get back."

~

MY FATHER SAW the play in Boston, which was lucky because it played a lot better there than it did in New York. Even though the play was a flop, it had to run for a minimum of three weeks. That part of it, I must admit, was rough—playing to a near-empty theater every night was a challenge. But as disappointed as I was, I never doubted the fact that I was good. I didn't want to be a star, I just wanted to act—and that's exactly what I was doing.

~

WHILE ALMA AND I were living our separate life on Broadway, Hitch was filming *Spellbound* (1945) for David O. Selznick. It was the first film he directed with Ingrid Bergman. The story was about a man (played by Gregory Peck) wrongly accused of murder, who, with the help of a lovely psychiatrist (Ingrid Bergman), engages in the search for the real killer. The film was one of the few of that era to deal with the field of psychiatry. It was an interesting story, full of visual possibilities. Daddy really had fun with that one, and some of the psychology foreshadows aspects of the story of *Marnie* that Daddy would do in 1964. The dream sequence in *Spellbound* was designed by Spanish artist Salvador Dali. Unfortunately, most of it would end up on the cutting room floor, never to be seen again. *Spellbound* had an Oscar-winning score by Miklos Rosza, and the film also marked the first collaboration between Daddy and legendary screenwriter Ben Hecht. Their friendship would carry over into the next picture, *Notorious* (1946), also starring Bergman, Cary Grant, and Claude Rains. Ingrid was very fond of my parents. I remember, she'd finish one film with Daddy and she'd come over, sit on the couch, and say, "When do we start the next one?"

～

Meanwhile, at the age of 16, I transferred for one year only to Marymount College in Tarrytown, New York. My parents threw a party for me before I left; Daddy, I remember, had a special gift for our guests: *Spellbound* perfume bottles. My most memorable day in school could have been fatal—and seemed to be straight out of one of my father's movies. I refer to it as "the trunk incident." One day, my friends and I were playing a game that required about twenty of us to hide, and the rest to go around and get people to sign a piece of paper. The one who gathered the most signatures won. I'm not sure whose idea it was, but I found myself hiding in a trunk that we had carried outside for the game. Later, we had to put it back where it belonged, and I enrolled my roommate to help me with it. She could not believe how I had managed to get inside the trunk, so I decided to demonstrate. I got in and the old-fashioned lock got stuck. Now, she might have locked me in, but I have no proof. When I asked her to open it, she tried but couldn't, so she panicked and started screaming. Everyone ran over to help, but no one could open the thing. I was screaming, "Break it open, I'll buy you a new one!" I remember hearing our chemistry teacher saying, "She has eighteen minutes of air left"; so at least I knew I was fine for a while. I must have been locked in there for at least ten minutes. Finally, this mystery man came and managed to open the trunk. My friends crowded around me when I came out. I never even found out who my savior was.

Years later, when my husband Joe and I were dating in New York, we got back to the hotel and there was a telegram that said, "Guess who got you out of the trunk, Love Bob." This seemed very strange to me and I kept wondering who it could be. When I told Joe the story, he said, "The only Bob I know is my brother-in-law." Though I knew there was no way it could've been the same Bob, we called him anyway, and sure enough it *was* him! At the time of the trunk incident, he had been taking his young cousins to school. He had heard all the yelling and ran to see what was happening. Because nobody else was able to do it, he'd figured he'd at least try and he pried the trunk open. Later on, he married Eileen, Joe's sister.

⁓

ALMA CALLED *NOTORIOUS* a classic the second she read the script. It was one of my father's few films from an original screenplay not based on any existing material. Ingrid Bergman played Alicia Huberman, the daughter of a spy, agreeing to go undercover for the Americans to frame Nazi conspirators. She makes many personal sacrifices, including marrying Alexander Sebastian (Claude Rains in one of his most amazing performances), the head of the organization. At the core of the story was the unresolved relationship our heroine has with the character played by Cary Grant, T. R. Devlin—her contact on the job. When Claude Rains discovers that his wife is an American agent, he and his devilish mother, Madame Sebastian (Leopoldine

Konstantin), decide to poison her. Luckily, she is saved by Devlin. One of the most famous sequences has to do with a wine cellar, where the villains hide the MacGuffin. In this case, it was some black powder that could possibly be used to make a bomb. Daddy and screenwriter Ben Hecht decided to research this and visited Dr. Robert Millikan at Cal Tech in Pasadena. Hitch asked if it would be possible to use uranium to build some sort of bomb. After picking himself off the floor, Dr. Millikan told them that was ridiculous. However, Daddy found out that his question had been more on target than he expected, and the FBI actually followed him and Ben Hecht for the next few months.

Alma was hired by *Shadow of a Doubt* producer Jack H. Skirball to co-write a comedy called *It's in the Bag* (1945). The film starred radio personality Fred Allen, Jack Benny, Don Ameche, William Bendix, and Robert Benchley. This madcap comedy was very much in the vein of Preston Sturges and W. C. Fields. It centered around a mystery successively making Allen a flea circus showman, the heir to a bunch of chairs (one of which contains a small hidden fortune), a murder suspect, and, finally, a hero. The reviews were very good—an article in the *New York Times* went as far as describing the plot as a mixture of Shakespeare and Alfred Hitchcock. The film was loosely based on an extremely popular Russian novel titled *The 12 Chairs,* which Mel Brooks would remake in the early seventies. *It's in the Bag* is extremely funny and displayed Alma's great talent for comedy. One amusing detail has to do with the opening credits. Jack Benny hosts the sequence, making silly remarks about everyone, including the screenwriters and said something like: "Don't pay attention to them—they never worked again." He was joking, of course, and Mama thought it was very funny, especially as she labored over the adaptation of Daddy's next film, *The Paradine Case* (1947). The credits listed David O. Selznick as screenwriter with Alma responsible for the adaptation of the novel by Robert Hichens. In looking through my parents' papers, I discovered that both another uncredited writer and Hitch himself had been involved with the script. I never found a script by David O. Selznick.

The film reunited my parents with Charles Laughton (who had appeared in *Jamaica Inn*), and this was their second picture with Gregory Peck after *Spellbound*. Ann Todd, who played Peck's wife, would become a good friend of my mother's. The film also starred Alida Valli as Mrs. Paradine, Louis Jourdan, Charles Coburn, Leo G. Carroll, and Ethel Barrymore. It was a court-room drama involving a rather naive defense attorney, Anthony Keane (Peck), who falls in love with his client, Mrs. Paradine (Valli), a woman accused of killing her husband. Blinded by his infatuation, Keane fails to realize that he is being manipulated by his client and nearly destroys his own marriage in the process. The truth of Mrs. Paradine's guilt comes out, and she is sentenced to death, while Keane realizes how much his wife loves him and repairs his marriage as well as his reputation. This was the last film Hitch did with Selznick. When they parted, Hitch had made only three films for him; the rest of the time he was on loan. Meanwhile, Daddy had been talking with his friend Sidney Bernstein about starting a production company. He was now free to realize that wish and, thus, was born Transatlantic Pictures in April of 1946, with offices both in London and in Burbank, and with Warner Brothers as their official distributor.

～⌒

I GRADUATED FROM Marymount High School, Los Angeles, in June 1947. Alma and Hitch sent out invitations to a party celebrating "The day on which Pat *hopes* to graduate." I knew that I wanted to study acting, but where was I going to college? At that time there were few colleges with good drama schools. The best one was the Catholic University in Washington, D.C. However, just to get in, one needed credits in theology, which I definitely did not have. I then decided to join the school of

Kenneth McGowan. He was a film theorist and teacher at UCLA, as well as a producer, author of several film textbooks, and an actor. I went over to UCLA to enroll, but I failed to bring with me the $12 for registration, so I left and went back home. Before I could even ask Daddy for the $12, he asked me if I would rather go to the Royal Academy of Dramatic Art (the famous RADA) in London! Would I ever! Mama took me to New York in January 1948 and put me on the *Queen Mary*. In London, I stayed with Mary and Teresa Hitchcock, two maiden elderly cousins of Daddy's who lived right outside London, in Golders Green. It was a great experience and one that certainly confirmed my passion for acting.

～

MAMA AND DADDY, OF course, kept busy while I was away. I'm not so sure I remember what Alma thought of *Rope* (1948). The way Daddy directed it was a bit unusual. He probably came up with this wacky idea at the dinner table after he and Alma had both read a play by Patrick Hamilton. The film was made around the time I was beginning at RADA and was Transatlantic Pictures' first production. The idea was to shoot the entire picture in twelve-minute takes. Each time the camera had to be reloaded, Daddy had devised to pan to someone's back or to a dark corner to hide the cuts and keep a seamless feeling. Hume Cronyn wrote a treatment based on the play, and Arthur Laurents wrote the screenplay. The story was very disturbing and loosely based on the Leopold/Loeb case (two young men who murdered a boy for the sheer challenge of it). The adaptation was a lot lighter and had irony to it, but it was still a rather dark and intense movie. The technique my father used on this film allowed for the audience to feel like they were right there, at the murder scene. *Rope* was also the first of several Hitchcock pictures to star James Stewart—an amazing man and a good friend. As the villains, Daddy cast John Dall and Farley Granger (with whom I would be in one of Daddy's finest films, *Strangers on a Train*).

Rope was a complete experiment and very difficult to shoot, for both the actors (who had to perform and move very precisely) and for the technicians (who had to make sure the camera traveled to the right spot at the right time, each time!). It was not huge at the box office, but today, it is one of my father's most memorable films because it was so unusual. He did try to duplicate the same camera technique—although not to such extreme—in his next picture, *Under Capricorn* (1949), a period piece starring our good friends Joseph Cotten and Ingrid Bergman. Ingrid, I seem to recall, was very frustrated with the way the film was being shot, but frankly, with Daddy, there was no room for discussion. However, while the film had interesting scenes, Daddy was just not as comfortable doing a period piece as making films in contemporary settings.

The story, which took place in Australia, circa 1830, did not mesh with the *Rebecca*-like plot of a woman terrorized in her own household. *Jamaica Inn,* another period piece, was also an unsuccessful picture. *Stage Fright* (1950), however, was a lot more fun to make; for one thing, it took place in England.

I remember meeting my parents when they got off the ship from America. I was thrilled to see them (and so happy that Mama had remembered to bring me my favorite white bread and rolls). I was very proud to share my accomplishments in school with them, and I felt very encouraged by my teachers. My student report for the spring term of 1948 speaks for itself:

"An excellent term work," one of my teachers wrote. "This student has a natural gift for comedy and avoids overplaying, which is most unusual in a first-term student. I was very pleased indeed with her performance of *Audrey.*"

"A good appreciation of performance and character," another teacher commented. "Blocks well and has a strong personality. A nice sense of comedy and timing."

I had to work particularly hard at my voice and at overcoming my American accent. How ironic!

～

I LOVED THE stage, but I also wanted to have film experience. So when Hitch and Alma began working on *Stage Fright* and told me that part of the story was set at RADA, I knew I was in luck. *Stage Fright* is about a young actress named Eve Gill (Jane Wyman) who falls in love with a man (Richard Todd) she believes was wrongly accused of murder. The film was quite disturbing, but it was treated very lightly and with a great deal of humor and style. For me, working on *Stage Fright* was an experience to be remembered—one of my idols, Marlene Dietrich, was in the film as Charlotte Inwood, a singer involved with the killer. She was quite wonderful and although we did not really have any scenes together, she would talk to me quite often and give me advice how I should be photographed. She would say, "Make sure they have the key light over there . . ." and I would think to myself, "Right, Marlene, they're going to care about what I tell them to do!" She was a sweet person and loved her family. She was also very easy to work with, because she knew what she was doing— a true professional. Jane Wyman played the lead in the film, and her character had quite a lot of driving to do. While the close-ups were shot on a sound stage, I was asked to be her double in the long shots, because you could not recognize her at the wheel. That way, if anything happened, Jane would be safe. Like my mother, I was a very good driver, and I was thrilled to be able to do anything on the film. My favorite time on the production was of course playing a friend of Jane Wyman during a garden party scene—my character's name was Chubby Bannister (no comment). I liked Jane Wyman very much; she was quite a character. One day, I went to see my parents at the Savoy and Jane, who was staying at that hotel as well, had a bad cold. She called me and said, "Come and see me." So I went. She was in bed, and we started chatting. She mentioned she had seen the musical show *South Pacific* and proceeded to sing the entire score. She was absolutely marvelous . . . although it was a bit strange, sitting there on her bed listening to her performing a musical! Speaking of musicals, I remember I once had to perform a comedic scene of my choice for school—and Mama suggested this number she had seen from *South Pacific* where Mary Martin washes her hair onstage while singing "I'm gonna wash that man right out of my hair." She thought it would be a great number to do in the comedy review. Unfortunately, she neglected to tell me that this took place in the shower! I, on the other hand, bent over a bowl filled with water, flooded the stage, and nobody could hear what I was singing.

~~~

STAGE FRIGHT WAS adapted by Alma, and the screenplay was written by Whitfield Cook (the author of the play *Violet*) based

Whitfield Cook, a good family friend Ann Chiesa, and Mama in Santa Cruz.

on the novel *Man Running* by Selwyn Jepson. Whitfield remembers: "I had a terrible cold, or the flu, and I got a call from Alma, asking if she and Hitch could come and see me; they had something to tell me. I said sure, but I don't think I can get out of bed. So Alma and Hitch came to see me and told me they wanted me to work on their next film, *Stage Fright* and of course, I was stunned! *Stage Fright* was the first film I wrote for Hitch and Alma—I'm happy to say that it holds up rather well and I can honestly say that it plays better now than it did when it first came out. When I was doing the screenplay, Hitch wanted Tallulah Bankhead to play the part of Charlotte Inwood, the actress/singer in the film. I immediately said, I don't think so, it should be someone glamorous like Marlene Dietrich. When the script was finished, Hitch talked to Jack Warner and presented five names—including Bankhead and Dietrich—and Warner said, there's only one choice, and that's Dietrich. And she got the part! She was amazing in the film. I particularly liked her at the end when she realizes she's been caught and doesn't lose her temper but tells this quick little story about a dog that bit her. She was just wonderful.

"One controversial aspect of the story was that it contained a flashback that turned out to be a lie: You actually saw a reenactment of the killer supposedly finding the body of the victim, whereas in fact, he was the murderer. That was Hitch's idea. I remember I didn't like this at first, and neither did Alma. But I could see why he liked it; to my knowledge, it had never been done before and it offered great visual possibilities. But I think we were criticized for it, and Hitch regretted doing it. Alma was credited for adapting Jepson's novel *Man Running,* and she was present at the story conferences. It was great to have her around because she had great opinions and was wonderful with structure. She knew and understood how films worked, and she understood almost as well as Hitch himself how suspense worked. Hitch was always the boss—but she wasn't the least bit afraid to give a different opinion. She could justify everything. And we both, Hitch and I, paid great attention to what she suggested.

"Even though we were close friends, we had a very honest working relationship. I never held anything from either Hitch or Alma for the sake of the friendship; in other words, I wasn't afraid of their reactions. There was mutual respect between us. On *Stage Fright,* Hitch, Alma, and I worked together for a while and then I went off on my own for three weeks to write the dialogue.

"When we were in England shooting, I wasn't needed much, so when she wasn't on the set or watching dailies, Alma would take me in her car around to the countryside. I remember we went to Oxford one day; another day she took me to Cambridge. It was the first time I had ever been to Europe, and I think it kind of amused both Alma and Hitch that I was new at traveling. They loved—especially Alma—showing me around.

"While we were in England, there was the scandal about Ingrid Bergman leaving her husband. Hitch had made several films with Ingrid, and both Alma and Hitch were crazy about her. Petter Lindstrom, her husband at the time, was a wonderful guy, but he was perhaps too immature for Ingrid. By now, she was already in Italy with the man who would become her next husband, filmmaker Roberto Rosselini—I think they were shooting their first film together—and Petter was on his way there to see what was going on with his marriage. He had a couple days in London, so Hitch wanted to take us all out to a famous pub. I had never been on the underground, so we went by subway and I remember the car was practically empty. It was Hitch, Alma, Petter, and I. Petter out of the blue said, 'You know, even with all this wiggling, I can still stand on my head.' And he did! And he thought it was a great thing to do. Hitch, Alma, and I just sat there watching him do his circus act. It was both very funny and unsettling.

Petter Lindstrom and Ingrid Bergman at our Santa Cruz home.

Petter Lindstrom with Mama and Daddy in the car behind him.

"I traveled throughout Europe while Hitch kept shooting and Alma would send letters, keeping me informed on the progress of the production. I remember she mentioned that Jane Wyman was a bit disappointed at the fact that Marlene Dietrich got to wear all those pretty clothes and she didn't; she had to look dowdy most of the time. Her role was definitely not glamorous—but she was so good in it! Alma's letters were always quite funny.

"When the film came out, it played at Radio City in New York. I don't know where Hitch was that night, but Alma and I went together to the opening and got a lot of attention from the management. It was great fun watching the movie with Alma because we would nudge each other about certain parts of the movie that worked and others that didn't. It was wonderful to see it with an audience because the comedy played a big role in the film—and people were laughing! The scenes between Jane Wyman and Alastair Sim (who played her father in the film) were particularly funny and went over quite well. The scene where Jane Wyman was trying to disguise herself and is immediately recognized by her mother was also quite hysterical and got a great reaction. I must say that both the leads and the supporting actors were, as customary in Hitch's films, very well cast and memorable.

"I loved going to parties at the Hitchcocks. You'd see Jimmy Stewart, Cary Grant, Bob Cummings, and Ingrid Bergman. There was also the amazing ranch up in Santa Cruz with acres and acres of land. It was beautiful—Alma and Hitch's bedroom was downstairs, and the guest rooms were upstairs. It was up on a little rise of land with a beautiful view. There was a little spot near the house they liked to go to for picnics, and that had an even better view. I was lucky to be up there on weekends. Alma was very comfortable around all the celebrities who were visiting them—she just took them in stride. It was great fun and very relaxing. We'd have good food, we'd play games—sometimes, we'd play Murder (a game where everyone has a piece of paper and one of them has the word 'Murderer' written on it; the goal is to find out who the killer is). Alma loved that game. Naturally, Hitch did, too.

"One day, I was up at the ranch and Alma and Hitch had read about a fancy recipe, something presented inside a coconut shell. So we took a ride into San Francisco to buy coconuts; we got back to the ranch and suddenly we realized that none of us could open them up. Hitch was standing at the kitchen sink in front of the window when he finally unexpectedly cracked one open; needless to say, all the milk went all over him. Alma and I had to help him get his suit off, and there he was, standing there in his underclothes. The house was at least two miles from the main road—it was very private—but at that very moment two ladies drove up. They were obviously lost—and quite shocked to get a glimpse of Hitch standing at the window in his underclothes! Hitch went to hide while Alma went out to tell the women they were trespassing. Alma did get to cook the coconut dish—and it was quite delicious!

"I was quite crazy about Alma because she was so gentle and yet so strong. I don't think she cared that people thought she was in the shadow of Hitch. She adored Hitch, and I know she loved working with him. Hitch and Pat were her life, and I don't recall, in the years that we were close, that she had friends of her own, for instance. Hitch and Alma always socialized *together*. But they were not interested in socializing in the Hollywood sense—I can remember one time they accepted an invitation to a New Year's Eve party at one of the big producer's houses; I was invited as well, and they were both bored to death."

To avoid being bored at his own parties, Daddy liked to pull pranks on his guests. I'll never forget one particular dinner party Hitch and Alma had organized. Everyone had arrived, including a little old lady who Hitch introduced as his mother visiting from England. Cary Grant, Ingrid Bergman, and everyone else were on their best behavior and were being very nice to Daddy's "mother." In reality, she was just someone Daddy had gotten through central casting. He played that joke, or variations of it, on several other occasions but to different crowds. He and Alma got such a great kick out of seeing all the bigwigs bowing to this little old lady! When he pulled that joke, Grandma had already been dead for several years.

1949–1959

FTER MY EXPERIENCE working with my parents on *Stage Fright,* I could not wait to do it again. The next opportunity came faster than I thought. *Strangers on a Train* (1951) was a great novel by Patricia Highsmith (the author of the acclaimed *Ripley* book series as well as many other novels). Although it would be changed quite a bit for the screen, the concept and spirit remained: Two men meet on a train and swap murders, but one is joking and the other is not and carries out his side of the deal. How could Daddy not love such an original setup?

Again, to Hitch and Alma's delight, Whitfield Cook came onboard to work on the adaptation:

"I adapted the novel, and Raymond Chandler did the script; Hitch also brought a woman named Czenzi Ormonde, who had worked for Ben Hecht. Writing the adaptation for me meant taking the book by Patricia Highsmith and working very closely with Hitch and Alma at changing a lot of things having to do with the setting and the plot. Hitch had some great ideas; for instance, he wanted the story to take place in Washington. The lead character was changed from an architect to a tennis player, and the whole twist at the end with the climax taking place in the amusement park was completely created for the film. The story begins with two men, Bruno Anthony and Guy Haines, meeting on a train and swapping murders; Bruno is to kill Guy's wife, and Guy, Bruno's father. Of course, Guy thinks this is just a joke, but Bruno doesn't and strangles Guy's wife. Guy is wrongly accused of the crime and has to confront Bruno in order to clear his name. When I started working on that project, I worked from the Hitchcock house, so logically Alma was involved from the beginning, even though, unlike *Stage Fright* and others, she didn't get credit. I loved to hear her thoughts on any of my ideas. Alma was very short but extremely attractive, and part of her attraction came through her intelligence and her warmth. During this second collaboration, I got to know Alma (and Hitch) even better; one thing I did notice about her was that she never talked about herself and she never talked about the past. She had been a pioneer in the silent era, but she never made a point of mentioning it.

"Hitch and Alma were very affectionate to one another—I remember later on when she got ill, people worried more about Hitch than they did about Alma! What would he do without her? He was petrified without her. He absolutely adored her.

"I cherish the fact that Hitch and Alma were witnesses at my wedding. My wife had nothing to do with the film industry—I met her on vacation on the Virgin Islands, and we were married in my house in Los Angeles. It was a very simple Presbyterian

service and then we all went to a restaurant I particularly liked, I think it was called La Rue (French for 'street'). Needless to say, my wife was completely bewildered by the whole thing. But Alma made her feel comfortable. I remember during dinner, when she had loosened up a little, my bride turned to Hitch and said, 'I noticed that you looked terribly solemn during the ceremony, what were you thinking?' And he said, 'I was thinking how well Whit's carpet has worn.' And he was serious because the next day, Hitch's secretary called and said he wanted to know where I bought my carpet!

"After *Strangers on a Train*, I didn't work again with Hitch and Alma, but on several occasions, I'd be in on discussions about other pictures they made. I remember they talked to me casually about *Rear Window* and how it was going to be seen from the point of view of one man in a cast, watching his neighbors across the way. And I said, that reminds me of when I had an apartment on West End Avenue in New York, and from the rear room of my apartment, I could see all this activity. There was one woman who had a little dog, and she was on the third floor.

So, in the morning she would let the little dog down in a basket, he would run around, go back in the basket, and she'd pull him up. Both Alma and Hitch thought that was a marvelous little vignette. They paid me about five thousand dollars so they could use it in the movie!

"I like to remember Alma as having fun and enjoying life. One evening, she called me and asked, 'Would you like to go dancing with Grace Kelly tonight?' I said, 'What do you think? I'm going to say no?' So off we went to one of the clubs on the strip, Hitch, Alma, Grace, and I!! I danced with Grace and Alma, who was herself quite a good dancer. Hitch just sat and watched.

"In 1966, I went to see Hitch and Alma in Saint Moritz for Christmas. They were staying at the Grand Hotel, and we (my wife, my son, and I) were staying at a charming small pension; when we got there, we were met at the station by a sleigh, and when we got to the little pension, there was this enormous bouquet of flowers from Alma and Hitch. They were so generous. In Saint Moritz, there were lots of things to do. The sun was so warm at times that you could go up the slopes and get a tan. We'd have lunch up there, then we'd come down and have hot chocolate at four o'clock, then have dinner. I'll never forget Alma saying, 'Hitch insists on getting into ski pants, which takes him about an hour, and then he sits on the porch smoking the whole time!' This sounds all very glamorous, but really, it was quite simple. The Hitchcocks lived well and never tried to impress anyone. A good example of that was the time Grace Kelly and her husband, Prince Rainier, came to visit them in Los Angeles. Alma set up the table in the kitchen! Of course, I think Hitch might have done this on purpose—he never quite forgave Grace Kelly for abandoning her acting career.

"Finally, Alma was truly a filmmaker. I can sincerely say from personal experience that I don't think Hitch's films would have been as good without Alma. He always went back to her. And frankly, so did I."

~⁓

THE GOOD NEWS for me on *Strangers on a Train* was that, this time, I had a much larger role. I played the sister of Ruth Roman who was romantically involved with Guy Haines (Farley Granger). My character's name was Barbara Morton (a slight improvement from Chubby Bannister, my name in *Stage Fright*). I was sort of the comic relief in this very grim situation, and the role gave me the opportunity to display my comic timing onscreen. On the set, I was not Hitch and Alma's daughter—I was one of the cast. I was treated equally to everyone else. I already knew some of the actors: Farley Granger and Leo G. Carroll, for instance. But I also got to know Robert Walker who was extremely charming and, I'm happy to say, not at all like Bruno Anthony, the intense psychotic character he played in the film. But like Norman Bates later in *Psycho* (1960), Bruno was a fascinating part in that he did not appear threatening at first. He was quite charming, funny, and stylish. Another resemblance to other Hitchcockian male characters was Bruno's strange relationship with his eccentric mother, delightfully played by Marion Lorne. She was completely oblivious to her son's mental sickness, and her ignorance, while being a sign of her own psychotic behavior, was also very amusing.

~⁓

STRANGERS ON A TRAIN offered great visual possibilities for my father, including the scene where the murder of Miriam, Guy's wife, takes place. The victim wears thick glasses, which fall to the ground as Bruno strangles her, and the murder is actually reflected in the glasses. The murder and the climax of the film were set in an amusement park. The final and deadly confrontation between Bruno and Guy takes place on a merry-go-round gone crazy. The shot of the merry-go-round falling apart was a combination of miniature work and shots done in front of a process screen. That scene is one of Daddy's greatest cinematic achievements. *Strangers on a Train* also marked the first of many films Daddy would do with the great cinematographer Robert Burks. They worked together from that day on (with the exception of *Psycho,* which was shot by Daddy's television crew), until Robert's untimely death in the mid-sixties.

Strangers on a Train also marked the beginning of an awful story that gets me upset each time I hear it, because it's always distorted. When I was not working, I would still go visit the set, and one day, Alma accompanied me to the amusement park that was built at the Warner Ranch in Woodland Hills. There, the story originated that Hitch was a sadistic father because he stuck me up on top of a Ferris wheel and left me there. Let the truth be known once and for all: I was afraid of heights, and Daddy asked me how much money I would want to go up on the Ferris wheel. I told him I would do it for a hundred dollars. I got on the ride with two boys from the film, and suddenly, the electricians below turned the lights off for all of two minutes. We came down, and the only sadistic part of this story is that I never got the hundred dollars. But many grabbed this incident and turned it into something distasteful. I really resent assumptions that have been written about both my parents. Of course, I know the truth, but it's frustrating to see how people love to rewrite history and turn a very innocent anecdote into something sensational.

～

AFTER *STRANGERS ON a Train,* I was in another play on Broadway, *The High Ground.* I also did several other films. I played a maid in an off-beat drama called *The Mudlark* directed by Jean Negulesco with Irene Dunne as Queen Victoria and Alec Guinness in 1950. I was so thrilled to meet and work with the great Alec Guinness—he could not have been nicer and was, in my mind, a true professional. He treated everyone on the set with equal respect and was always gracious. I had the opposite experience working with Cecil B. de Mille on *The Ten Commandments*. I had such a tiny part, I was practically an extra, but it was enough for me to observe that de Mille was extremely difficult to work with. His sets were very different from my father's. De Mille ran his like a drill sergeant. On *The Ten Commandments*, there was this other girl I was hanging out with, and after we finished our four-day bit, she said, "I'm going to go up and thank Mr. de Mille for using me." I couldn't believe she could just walk up to him, but she did. She thanked him, and because he was so flattered, he kept her on the film for two additional months.

In general, being the daughter of Alfred Hitchcock did not necessarily open doors for me when I was looking for acting work. I think people had a tendency to think, "Her father is in the business, that's how she got started as an actress." They never really wanted to give me a chance to show that I really had talent. I was at peace with the situation, although at times, it was quite frustrating and discouraging. I never complained about it, but my parents knew that it wasn't easy for me.

～

IN THE SPRING of 1951, I spoke to Alma and explained I wanted to go to Maine, a place I had never been. Ten minutes later, Hitch called to say that he had a few weeks to spare before starting to work on his new script, *I Confess* (1953), and why didn't I put my car on the ship and join them for the trip? I agreed, not realizing that I would meet my future husband on that ship: *The Saturnia*. Joseph E. Connell was a dashingly handsome businessman from New England. He was born in Boston on August 4, 1927, and came from a large Irish Catholic family. He also was the grandnephew of the late Cardinal O'Connell of Boston. At the time we met, he was the treasurer of the Thomas Dalby Corporation of Watertown, Massachussetts. He was traveling with one of his sisters (he had three) and his father, who had

My husband-to-be Joe O'Connell, Daddy, me, Joe's father Joe, Sr., Mama, and Joe's sister Cappy.

been a widower for a year. We were going to many of the same places in Europe, and we all had a marvelous time. Meanwhile, sitting at the same table as the O'Connells was the young lady who became very important to Joe's father. In Paris, at the Coq Hardi Restaurant, Joe's father told Alma that he was going to remarry. He was already very comfortable with Alma and wanted her in the confidence. In this (undated) letter to Carol Stevens, Mama talks of the trip from the luxurious Hotel Plaza Athenée in Paris:

My dear Carol,

Just a few lines to let you know how and where we are. It is just heavenly here—really Paris in the spring. We have been so lucky with the weather. Usually the rains cleared about two days before we arrived at various places. It was rather cold at Capri, but lovely in the sun. Pat drove from Naples to Rome. It had been raining in Rome for weeks, but had cleared up two days before. We saw a great deal of

Ingrid [Bergman]—I'll tell you more about her when we get back. The baby [Bergman's] is just sweet! Rossellini [Roberto Rossellini, Bergman's husband] was in Paris, thank goodness. Ingrid is very thin, almost gaunt. Smartly dressed, jewelry, etc. So on first appearance she strikes you as being hard. She seemed very pleased to see us, and once the first strain was over, it wasn't so bad. She seems to talk incessantly and speaks Italian fluently. I drove from Rome to Florence. Florence we just loved. We didn't have much time there. Only one night and next morning. It has been very badly damaged during the war. So many places have, it is very sad. Pat then drove to Venice. That's about the same. Quite attractive, but, oh, it is so smelly in the back canals and alleys. It really gets right down on one's stomach. We met [actor] Lew Ayres and his wife there. Pat then drove to Innsbruck. We had the night there and left the next morning. Had a wonderful drive through Bavaria. Saw Berchtesgarten, where Hitler used to live, etc. We had that night at Salzburg. It was rather depressing there, but strange to see the place swarming with American troops. All that section is in the American zone. Next on to Munich. That was really very sad. As you know, we lived there some time. It has been smashed up badly. I'm afraid I'm giving you a very sketchy idea of our travels, but you can see how we've been moving. In Munich Pat decided to fly to Berlin. It seemed such a shame for her not to see it when we were in that part of the world. Hitch and I drove on to Strasbourg, then on here [Paris] and met Pat. She had a very exciting time, introductions to an American flying man there, and also some English press correspondents. She certainly has appreciated this trip. I am so glad we brought her; she is so thrilled by everything. We have been going very carefully with money, and until we came here we were in pretty good shape. Things are very expensive in Paris generally, food, etc. . . . so much more than anywhere else, but we are counting the pennies and really watching our step. We expect to go over to London about next Monday, the 23rd and only plan to be there a week, but we'll let you know any change of plans later. Did you get Mr. H's letter? We thought that was best about the settee. It seems a shame to rush into buying the covering unless we really liked it. I'd sooner keep it a little longer till we find something we like. I hope everything is alright with you, and that you are feeling better now. Please remember me to Sherry, and save up all those pennies, so you can take a trip like this, it's well worth it.

Love from us all, Alma.

~⌒

THE O'CONNELLS took the *Queen Elizabeth* home. My parents and I flew to Canada and drove my car through the East Coast, stopping off in Boston to visit the O'Connells. The last time I had been there was for the opening of *Violet*. It was one of Mama's favorite cities.

After my parents returned to Los Angeles, I stayed in New York to further my career doing radio and live television. In September of 1951, Joe and I announced our engagement. I had already told Alma (she was the first to know); she was thrilled, and so was Daddy. The announcement was made public in the press:

"Mr. and Mrs. Alfred J. Hitchcock of Los Angeles and Santa Cruz, Cal., announce the engagement of their daughter, Patricia, to Joseph E. O'Connell Jr., son of Joseph E. O'Connell and the late Mrs. O'Connell of Newton and West Hyannisport.

"Miss Hitchcock is a graduate of Marymount High School, Los Angeles, and the Royal Academy of Dramatic Art in London, England. Her father is the noted film director.

"Mr. O'Connell was graduated from Georgetown Preparatory School in Garrett Park, Md., and served in the Navy during World War II. He is a grandnephew of the late William Cardinal O'Connell of Boston and is treasurer of the Thomas Dalby Corporation in Watertown."

JOE AND I decided to get married on the East Coast, as I had many friends there and Joe had a lot of family in Boston. We were married at Our Lady Chapel in Saint Patrick's Cathedral in January 1952, and the Rt. Rev. Msgr. Jeremiah F. Minihan of Boston officiated. "When he gave the bride away," Mama once wrote in an article titled "My Husband Alfred Hitchcock Hates Suspense," "Hitch's face was so white that a member of the groom's family remarked that he must have just come out of a

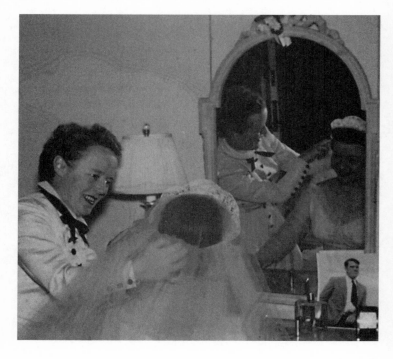

Hitchcock movie." My wedding was one of the happiest days of my life. I was nervous of course, but just so happy to be starting a life with Joe. I wore a gorgeous gown of cream nylon tulle in the bouffant style with short train and an off-the-shoulder neckline edged with Alençon lace. My headdress, a small tiara of the lace, held a medium-length veil of the same tulle, and I carried a prayer-book with a marker of orchids. Alma had chosen an oyster faille dress with jet black buttons down the front and black accessories. Daddy had on a stylish tuxedo. Joe's sister Cappy O'Connell was our maid of honor; John Baldwin, a very close friend of Joe's, was best man. Ushers were Robert J. Cunningham, William J. Keville Jr. (both were Joe's brothers in law), and Reuben Dunsford, another one of Joe's friends. A reception was held at the St. Regis Roof at the St. Regis Hotel in New York following the ceremony. Although, we had been celebrating the entire week: a supper hosted by Whitfield Cook, a cocktail party given by Mr. and Mrs. James Barrett, and a dinner given by Joe's father and his second wife.

~

WE HAD OUR honeymoon in Havana, and we had already planned to move to Los Angeles when we returned. Alma had taken my dog, a miniature Sealyham, back home. However, it was not to be—the company Joe worked for cancelled their initial intention to send a representative to the West Coast. Subsequently, Joe got a job at CBS in the mail room—not quite what we had planned. Meanwhile, I continued to do a lot of live television. When I found out I was pregnant with my first child, I flew to Quebec to tell my parents, who were filming *I Confess*. On April 17, 1953, Mary Alma O'Connell was born, right after we had finally made the move to Los Angeles. I would have two other daughters: Teresa (Tere) born July 2, 1954, and Kathleen (Katie), born February 27, 1959. "We were a family of seven," Mary says, "Dad, Mom, three daughters, Alma, and Hitch. Every birthday, holiday, and vacation were practically spent together.

The holidays became even more special to my parents, my husband and myself after our daughters were born.

Alma and Hitch loved my father and got along with him famous-ly. It was a very loving and respectful relationship. And when my father had two open heart surgeries in the seventies, Alma and Hitch were extremely helpful and supportive. The family spirit was as important to my father as it was to Alma and Hitch."

~

WHILE I WAS starting my new life, Alma and Hitch were very busy on *I Confess.* The premise was about a priest who knows the identity of a killer but cannot reveal it because he learned it in confession. As always, my mother was very involved with all aspects of the production, beginning with the script adaptation of the play *Nos Deux Consciences (Our Two Consciences)* by Paul Anthelme. The film had already been in development prior to Daddy's involvement, and Alma was very instrumental in sorting out the pre-existing screenplays and in selecting with Hitch a writer to do a new adaptation. (It was pure coincidence that the killer's wife in the film was named Alma!) Mama then traveled to Quebec for the early location scouting and stayed on when shoot-ing began. *I Confess,* the third of five films Daddy would direct for Warner Brothers, had a great cast but wasn't a very happy expe-rience. Karl Malden as Inspector Larrue was a delight, as was Anne Baxter, who played the love interest and spent a lot of time with Mama visiting the Canadian countryside on her off days. The problem was the lead, Montgomery Clift. When my hus-band and I visited the location to tell my parents that I was preg-nant, Daddy was filming an intense scene with actor O. E. Hasse, who played the killer. The next shot required Monty Clift to sim-ply walk across a large ballroom—and he just sat there to think and think about it. He was holding everybody up, and Daddy became very impatient.

The film was not very well received; I personally think that it was not as visually exciting as Daddy's previous pictures and like *The Paradine Case,* for instance, and it did not really have humor or irony as so many other titles of my father's had. But again, the event of the year was the fact that Hitch and Alma were going to be grandparents. Alma was particularly support- ive. She was almost as excited as if she was having the baby her- self! The truth is, Alma was always so youthful that she com- pletely identified with me. She never treated me like a daughter, but more like a sister. My friends loved her—to most of them, she was like *their* mother!

My close friend Georgia Waller remembers: "Some of the most glamorous and exciting memories of my life revolve around Alma Hitchcock and her daughter, Pat. It has been more than fifty years since Pat and I graduated from Marymount High School (class of '47). In retrospect, it's hard to believe we have been friends for more than half a century. Alma was a real lady in her manner, habits, and style. Her priority was her fam- ily, next came the dogs and her home. Alma and Hitch were per- fect together—and perfect hosts I might add, to Pat's friends such as myself. What is most interesting to me is that, having observed Hitch and Alma, I recognized the same commitment in Pat toward her husband Joe. Pat and Alma were both devot- ed to their respective husbands—but both kept their independ- ence, their opinions, and their personality."

My dear and best friend Louie Ramsay, whom I met at RADA, has an interesting anecdote showing yet another side of Alma's wonderful personality: "I was staying with the Hitchcock family in 1949. Pat had stayed with my family during part of the time we were in school and then, of course, I was invited out to Los Angeles. The family home was in the beauti- ful area of Bel Air that backed into a golf course. One day, I was looking out of the window and suddenly, I realized Clark Gable was playing—and missing a putt! I ran through the house look- ing for Alma—Pat and Hitch were out, and told her that I had just seem my idol, Clark Gable. Then, the unexpected hap- pened; Alma said, 'Come on, follow me!' We ran out the back door, down a narrow alleyway, and cut through what seemed to be someone else's backyard. Finally, we emerged from a hedge, and there we were on the eighteenth green. Out of breath, a little disheveled, but there. Alma just gave quick instructions: 'Pretend we're just out for a walk.' And suddenly, we were facing Gable and Alma was introducing me to him! For an eighteen-year-old aspiring actress, that was quite a moment, and I owe it all to Alma!"

As I mentioned earlier, despite the fact that we were so near a golf course, Daddy and Mama did not play golf (I did and still do). But both of them enjoyed watching tennis—Alma I recall also had a preference for boxing. She did not like heavy-weight, but middle-weight boxing! Who would have thought!

~

ALMA WAS VERY close with many of the actresses who worked with Hitch. But she definitely had a soft spot for Grace Kelly. The first of three films Hitch did with Grace was *Dial M for Murder* (1954). It was based on a play by Frederick Knott about a husband whose plan to have his wife murdered by another man backfires when she stabs the killer in self-defense. Unfortunately, it looks like the wife, who was having an affair with another man, deliberately murdered her assailant because, the police assume, he was blackmailing her. But the truth prevails and the husband eventually gets caught for staging the whole thing. There had been a BBC broadcast of the play in 1952. I know Daddy wasn't particularly thrilled with the film— he used to say, "I telephoned this one in," meaning he did not need to show up on the set. But I suspect Hitch might have just been trying to make a pun when he said that. *Dial M for Murder* is a great suspenseful film; it's not as good as the next one (*Rear Window*), but it's an honorable precursor. Although there are a couple scenes staged outside the apartment where the crime is committed in *Dial M for Murder*, *Rear Window* and *Dial M*, like

Rope take place in one location. The other interesting thing about the film was that it was shot in 3-D. I remember watching the film wearing those ridiculous 3-D glasses but being petrified, especially during the murder sequence. There is one shot where Grace Kelly is being strangled and her hand reaches out and grabs a pair of scissors; it was just horrifying but I couldn't help but watch (that was part of Daddy's genius).

The film also starred Ray Milland, our good friend Robert Cummings, and John Williams (who would later star in *To Catch a Thief* (1955) and in several episodes of the *Alfred Hitchcock Presents* television series). Toward the end of the shooting, Hitch met a young man named Herbert Coleman, who would become an associate for many years to come. As with many of the people he hired in front of and behind the camera, Hitch always felt they had to pass the ultimate test: the Alma test. Herbie went to my parents' house after his initial meeting with Hitch on the set of *Dial M*. Alma welcomed him with a broom in one hand and a waste basket in the other. Herbie confessed he immediately loved Alma. The meeting was casual, with Hitch showing his art collection and Alma asking questions about Herbie's family and his wife. Herbie passed away in 2001, but he remained a close friend of mine and, like Charles Bennett, was one of the few who always made sure Alma's name was mentioned in the same breath as Hitch's.

Around the time Hitch made *Dial M*, Lew Wasserman, Daddy's agent at MCA (who would later become the head of Universal), got him a very lucrative contract at Paramount. Lew was one of the great inspirational forces in my father's career. They were very close friends as well and socialized on many occasions. He subsequently advised my daughters and myself on many occasions, with the same intelligence and creativity he had shared with Daddy and Mama.

The first film under this new contract would be a true masterpiece, *Rear Window* (1954). A news photographer, L. B. Jeffries

(James Stewart), is in a cast after an accident and starts observing his neighbors across the way. One of them (Raymond Burr), he suspects, might have killed his wife. With the help of his eager-to-please girlfriend (Grace Kelly), who is hoping for a ring in exchange for her snooping, and his eccentric nurse (Thelma Ritter), Jeffries discovers that, indeed, the neighbor is guilty of murder. The case is solved, but Jeffries is nearly killed in his attempt to frame the murderer. Luckily, instead, he just ends up with yet another broken leg! The premise was based on a short story (*It Had to Be Murder*) by Cornell Woolrich (also known as William Irish), and the screenplay was by John Michael Hayes (who would collaborate with Daddy on a total of four films). According to him, "Alma was pure sunshine. She advised Hitch on everything. She kept him balanced and approached everything with good humor, she was very thoughtful and always nice. I was very fond of her."

Of all the sets to visit of my father's movies, *Rear Window* was by far, as Mama would have agreed, the most fascinating one. Alma would often call me and say, "You've got to come to the studio and see the sets!" She was very enthusiastic and never seemed jaded, even after so many years of working in the business; each new film with Hitch meant new excitement. On *Rear Window*, the entire apartment and the view of the neighbors was built on Paramount's Stage 18. It looked so real, I literally felt like I had been transported to Greenwich Village. *Rear Window* is Hitchcock 101—you have the anti-hero, the cool blonde, the humor, a grisly murder, a love story, and dialogue about food. The film is brilliant because it puts the audience in the position of the voyeur. It has since been imitated by many filmmakers but never equaled. The picture was a huge success both with critics and with audiences around the world; even today, the film does not have one wrinkle and still seems very modern.

One reason the film was so classy is that it reunited Hitch with famous costume designer Edith Head. Edith had worked on

Notorious, but on *Rear Window,* her role and contribution became vital. As I said earlier, the costumes were often part of the plot, so Ms. Head had to be involved very early on. In the later years, she would develop wardrobes for the public appearances of Tippi Hedren, for instance, when she was touring for *The Birds* and *Marnie.* Edith also designed clothes for Alma, very smart yet simple outfits.

Understandably, Alma and Hitch were thrilled when the opportunity of doing *To Catch a Thief* (1955) came up. It seemed to capture so much of what the Hitchcock spirit was all about. With exteriors shot on the French Riviera and a plot featuring a costume ball, everyone involved with the production worked frantically with Daddy to make the film a glamorous feast for the eyes. And it worked so well, director of photography Robert Burks received an Oscar for Best Color Cinematography. The film was shot in VistaVision, a new revolutionary process created by Paramount that completely magnified the beauty of the locations—and of the actors! Mama was also quite present during the production; for instance, she outlined the car chase scene—a pivotal moment in the film. The way the scene was originally written involved too much lengthy dialogue, and it was Alma who suggested breaking it all into three different scenes—that way, the audience was kept alert and interested. *To Catch a Thief* was based on a novel by David Dodge and was written by John Michael Hayes. The film starred Grace Kelly, the dashing Cary Grant (at his best playing a retired jewel thief who is framed by a copycat), Jessie Royce Landis as Grace's extravagant mother, and our good friend John Williams as a jewel insurance agent. *To Catch a Thief* was pure fun and treated almost like a madcap comedy. One reason was the witty dialogue, loaded with double-entendres. A classic example is the scene where Grace and Cary are having a picnic. Grace offers: "A leg or a breast?" She is referring, of course, to the cold chicken. Or is she? The dynamics between Grant and Kelly as well as Jessie Royce Landis' hilarious performance place the film not so much as a thriller, but as pure entertainment and as one of Hitch's best. The film was a stunning success, but, unfortunately, it would be the last Hitchcock film to star Grace Kelly. She became a Princess in 1956 when she married Prince Rainer III of Monaco. They did not meet during the production of *To Catch a Thief,* but a year later when Grace returned to the south of France for Cannes Film Festival.

My parents traveled around the world to promote the film. Selling the pictures was always part of the job, and Alma was there, at Hitch's side, offering support and making sure things went smoothly. Most memorable was the Royal premiere at the Odeon Theatre in London on Monday October 31st, 1955, in the presence of Her Majesty, the Queen, and H.R.H. The Duke of Edinburgh. Special dress code was required: full evening dress, no accessories, no gloves for gentlemen, white gloves for ladies.

At one point on the tour, I was called by a reporter from the *Los Angeles Times,* who asked if I knew that my parents' plane had not yet arrived in Singapore and was basically missing. It was a frightening day. My husband Joe had gone to a football game at the Los Angeles Coliseum and came out at half time and saw the headlines "Hitchcock Missing!" He immediately left and raced home. We were both completely scared of what might have happened, and all kinds of thoughts raced through our minds. And then, at eight in the evening, the same reporter who had initially contacted me called back to inform us that my parents had been found and were safe. Their plane had been delayed on the runway in Bangkok, and no one had bothered sending a message to inform of the delay.

～

AS I MENTIONED earlier, Alma always kept her British accent. While Hitch lost his, he never lost his British sense of humor. And with *The Trouble with Harry* (1955), as Alma and others often said, Hitch made his most British movie. The story was based on a book by Jack Trevor Story with a screenplay by John Michael Hayes. *Harry* is the story of a dead body and those who come in contact with him. Even though the movie did poorly, it remained one of my parents' favorites. The film reunited my parents with their old friend Edmund Gwenn, but it also introduced them to Shirley MacLaine (in her screen debut) and to the very talented John Forsythe (who would work again with Daddy on *Topaz* in 1969). Mama and Daddy went to Vermont to shoot the exteriors, and Alma sent me a cookbook, *Vermont's Kitchen*, from there—I still have it. The shooting on location was a bit rough. It was fall and the countryside was just beautiful when they first arrived. Then, they were hit by a storm that stripped all the trees. In consequence, some of the exteriors had to be re-created on a soundstage—and all the leaves had to be shipped in giant crates from Vermont to Paramount.

One of the characters in the film was the music, and on *Harry*, Hitch got a chance to collaborate with composer Bernard Herrmann for the first time. Herrmann wrote the most delicious

themes for the film, including a suite he later titled *A Portrait of Hitch*. Bernie Herrmann and Hitch would collaborate on many other pictures—even one without music, *The Birds* (1963), for which Herrmann would design the bird sound effects. In 1955, the year *Harry* was released, Hitch finally decided to become a U.S. citizen, five years after Alma. I guess it took him a bit longer to make up his mind. The ceremony took place on April 20, 1955. Alma was pleased that they were now fully committed to their adoptive nation.

ONCE *HARRY* WAS completed, Hitch was asked by our good friend Lew Wasserman to do a television series for CBS, *Alfred Hitchcock Presents*. Lew had been Daddy's agent since Myron Selznick's death in 1945. After discussing it with my mother, he thought it over and agreed. He set up a company called Shamley Productions, naming it after our country home in England, and he brought in Joan Harrison as producer. Joan then hired Norman Lloyd to be associate producer. (After five years, Norman would become producer and then executive producer of the series.) They immediately began to look for short stories with a twist and collaborated with very talented screenwriters and directors on the rise to adapt the material to the (small) screen. Hitch agreed to direct some of the episodes, and I would act in some of them—although none of the ones directed by my father. The star of the show was Hitch himself—with his famous lead-ins and his jokes about "his sponsors"; they were written by James Allardice, who would also collaborate with Hitch on the trailers in which he appeared. (For *Psycho*, rather than showing excerpts from the film, Hitch took the audience on a guided tour of the Bates Motel.)

With the huge success of Daddy's films and the upcoming television series, Hitch and Alma couldn't go anywhere without being recognized. My daughters were particularly uncomfortable with the kind of attention their grandfather got from complete strangers. Hitch, of course, had a great sense of humor about it. He'd be driving with my daughters, and someone would pull up next to him, waving. He'd turn to the kids nonchalantly and say, "Friends of yours?" My daughter Mary specifically remembers going with him to see *Swan Lake* and during the intermission, people crowded all around them just to talk to Hitch. My daughters have always said they loved going out with their grandfather, but they were amazed at all the attention he got when seen in public. As they got older, they got used to it. As for my mother, she felt it was part of the job. They were both very nice about it, and Daddy was really great to fans; one day, we were all eating at Perino's, a hot spot in Hollywood, and someone walked up to our table and asked for his autograph. My daughter Tere asked Daddy, "Doesn't it bother you?" He replied, "This is my audience. Without them, I'd be nothing."

Hitch had become a brand name and even created a magazine, *The Alfred Hitchcock Mystery Magazine* (I was the associate editor). The first episode of *Alfred Hitchcock Presents* aired on October 2, 1955. *Revenge* was directed by Daddy, and starred Vera Miles. Two hundred sixty-five shows would follow. Daddy did not direct all of them—only several of the best ones—but he did introduce all of them. In 1962, Daddy would create another series titled *The Alfred Hitchcock Hour*, of which there would be 93 episodes. Shamley Productions also did other television series: *Suspicion* for NBC, and one dramatic presentation called *Ford Startime*.

My daughter Mary recalls: "My 'grandma,' as my sisters and I called her, was always very loving and supportive of us. She had a great interest in our lives whether it be our schoolwork or our friends. We were always very comfortable bringing our friends into their home. She always made them feel welcome.

"When I was seven years old I was cast in a very, very small part on one of the *Alfred Hitchcock Presents* shows. The story was called 'The Schartz-Metterklume Method' and was directed by Richard Dunlap. The original airdate was June 12, 1960. Norman Lloyd thought it would be fun to have three generations of Hitchcocks involved with this episode. My mom had a part in this show as she had had on a number of the other episodes. This was to be my first and only time. My grandmother made sure that I had a good experience. It was certainly not something she would have encouraged. She felt children should live their lives as children and not as actors. But, she felt this one experience was great fun for me. Everyone made sure I had a wonderful time for the couple of days that I was there. I enjoyed it very much. However, when the episode was finished it was back to being a 'regular' child again, something that my grandparents felt very strongly about."

But amidst all those projects, Hitch was having trouble finding his next feature film, and, after his usual discussions about it with my mother, he finally settled on a remake of one of his own, *The Man Who Knew Too Much* (1956), starring Doris Day and Jimmy Stewart. Daddy always said that the original version was done by an amateur, and the remake by a professional. The picture, written by John Michael Hayes, started on location in Morocco and ended in London at Albert Hall during a concert conducted by none other than Bernard Herrmann himself!

The film marked Hitch's first official collaboration with production designer Henry Bumstead—whom we all call Bummy: "After we had worked on *The Man Who Knew Too Much*, Hitch called me one day and said he wanted me to do a room for him at his home on Bellagio Road. He had bought a carpet over in Marrakesh, and he wanted me to do all kind of work, and it turned out beautifully. And I never heard a word from Hitch until one morning I was going to work and I saw Alma. She used to drive Hitch to the studio and had a little Thunderbird. And Alma said, 'How are you doing, Bummy?' and we got talking.

Daddy and I on the set of The Man Who Knew Too Much.

She said, 'You know that room you did for us turned out beautifully.' And I said, 'Well, I wondered how you felt about it.' She said, 'Didn't Hitch ever say anything?' And I said, 'Not a word.' 'Why,' she says, 'that old. . . .' Later, when I got to my office, my secretary said, 'Mr. Hitchcock wants to see you immediately.' So I went down to see Hitch. And he was all smiles and said, 'Didn't I ever thank you for the work you did at the house?' And I said

'No, you didn't.' He said, 'Well, it turned out beautifully. Thank you.' Hitch a good sense of humor. That was a nice moment with him. All thanks to Alma."

⁓

THE MAN WHO *Knew Too Much* was a big success, both my parents were delighted and thrilled that their instincts to remake the British version had been right. On the occasion of the release of the film, Daddy wrote an article about Mama titled— appropriately—"The Woman Who Knows Too Much":

"Alma is most extraordinary in that she's normal. Normality is becoming so unnormal these days. She has a consistency of presence, a lively personality, a never-clouded expression and she keeps her mouth shut except in magnanimously helpful ways. She's aware that I become paralyzed with fear at the sight of a cop, but rather than try to analyze me, a method through which more wives than one have demolished otherwise honorable husbands: Alma cheerfully offers to do most of the driving.

"Alma knows much—too much—about me. But Alma isn't talking. She knows that for a thriller-movie-making ogre, I'm hopelessly plebian and placid. She knows that instead of reading mysteries at home I'm usually designing a built-in cupboard for the house; that I wear conservative clothes and solid-color ties; that I prefer talkative colors to somber ones in a room, properly introduced through flowers or fine paintings. She knows I share her tastes for modest living, but that my tendency to utter terrible puns makes me a trial to live with. She knows how relieved we were, in a way, when our daughter settled her movie career for one part in *Strangers on a Train*, then decided that being a mother of sticky-fingered children required all her creative attention.

"Next to policemen, I dread being alone. Alma knows that, too. I simply like the woman's presence about, even if I'm reading. She puts up with a lot from me. I dare say any man who names his dog Phillip of Magnesia, as I did, is hard to live with. Alma won't say.

"It isn't my fault, really, that Alma has stayed so much out of sight of the public, although I suspect I'm accused a lot of over-shadowing her. She does read for me and I rely on her opinion. She helped work out on paper the chase scene in *To Catch a Thief.* She's always on the set the first day we begin shooting a film, sometimes goes to rushes, and always gives me her criticisms. They're invariably sound. She still knows the business well, which proved handy again when I began to produce my Sunday television show for CBS.

"Alma thinks it's a shame I've been typed as a mere maker of suspense and murder movies. But I'm afraid to risk too 'offbeat' a movie; people wouldn't like it because I did it. 'It wasn't good Hitchcock,' the critics would say.

"In many ways it's a nuisance having a wife who knows all this but won't talk. The inherent danger is that the husband will never be talked about in public. It, in fact, eventually imposes upon him the egoistic need to write about himself. I'm sure I prefer it that way. I suspect Alma knows that, too."

∼

HITCH WAS FASCINATED with real-life mysteries. Alma was, too. But few of the films were based on fact; perhaps that's why they were so entertaining. In looking for something drastically different from his previous work, Hitch settled on *The Wrong Man* (1956), based on the true story of a musician wrongly accused of a crime and how it shattered his family. It was a serious take on one of Daddy's most recognizable themes. (The story had been produced on television for NBC by Robert Montgomery in 1953.) For the film, and given the nature of the story, Daddy decided not to do his usual cameo appearance. Hitch actually had filmed a scene in which he did a cameo, but he decided to take it out due to the seriousness of the story.

Instead, he introduced the story at the beginning of the film, explaining that this time, he was dealing with real life and that *The Wrong Man* was a serious true story. Though my father spent his career experimenting and we accept his films today because they're part of cinema, back in the days when he decided to do *The Wrong Man*, he was taking a chance, especially because audiences were used to his tongue-in-cheek style. Mama was also very supportive of his choice to do something as daring as *The Wrong Man*. It was a very shocking, very depressing movie because it was real. The script was written by Maxwell Anderson and Angus MacPhail and based on the *Life* article "A Case of Identity" by Herbert Brian. Henry Fonda was absolutely heartbreaking in the role of this struggling man who gets confused for a criminal, and Vera Miles, as his wife who goes mad because of it, was a revelation. Daddy liked her so much (she had also done a brilliant episode of Daddy's series titled "Breakdown") that he signed a contract with her. Unfortunately, Vera got pregnant and Daddy had to look for a new star for his next film, *Vertigo* (1958).

～

WHILE MY FATHER was shooting episodes of his television show, he discovered a French novel titled *From Amongst the Dead* by Pierre Boileau and Thomas Narcejac. The story was about a man who witnesses the death of the woman he loves. Later, he sees someone who looks exactly like her—and finds out that she is the same person. The man discovers that he was framed and had witnessed not a suicide, but a murder. The plot was very convoluted, and it took a lot of work to adapt the book to an American setting. The credited screenwriters were Alec Coppel and Samuel Taylor. But while developing the story, Hitch was not feeling well, and on January 17, 1957, he finally had to check into the hospital for an operation. While his doctor did not regard the operation as serious, it was essential.

Daddy had had the hernia for years, but it never caused him any trouble until that winter, when he suffered pain. So he decided to just have surgery rather than risk having an attack when he was making a picture or a TV show. My mother and I were very confident that he would have no difficulty, especially since Daddy himself was pretty cheerful. But by March, Hitch had to be rushed to the hospital again, this time for something more serious. His gallbladder had to be removed. Now Hitch was terrified but tried to keep his spirits up. "I suffered two internal hemorrhages," he explained to a journalist. "I was told that this often happens to people and not to worry. So I wasn't alarmed. But they told my wife she had better see a priest." Once Hitch felt better, it was back to work as usual.

~

VERTIGO MAY BE a classic today, but it wasn't when it was first released. Again, I think Daddy was experimenting, and even though he had the likes of Jimmy Stewart and the glamour of Kim Novak, the film was perhaps ahead of its time. People did not accept the dark ending and did not really understand the journey of a man obsessed with recreating the image of a woman he lost. When Hitch was rejected by the critics, he claimed he did not care. Being rejected by the public was disappointing. But any negative comments from Alma were to him the most devastating. "I was told a story by Peggy Robertson, Hitch's assistant," said filmmaker Peter Bogdanovich (who wrote a great deal about Hitch). "Alma saw the film after it was completed. She and Hitch were riding in the car on the way back home, and Alma was just raving about the picture, saying that it was wonderful, one of his best. But she added: 'There's one shot of Kim Novak crossing the street I think you should take out. She looks a little broad in the beam—or something like that. But you know Hitch, the film is just wonderful.' Later, Peggy was alone with Hitch, and Hitch was completely silent.

So Peggy said, 'Isn't it wonderful Alma loves the film?! What's the matter Hitch, you don't seem happy.' and Hitch said, 'Alma hates the picture.' And it was all because she had this one little criticism. He got very upset if she didn't like something."

~~~

AROUND THE TIME that *Vertigo* was released, on April 12, 1958, Mama found out she had cancer of the uterus. When she came home with the news, Daddy was totally devastated. I knew I had to stay strong for the both of them. That very night, my parents already had dinner plans with *Vertigo* screenwriter Samuel Taylor and his wife, so rather than cancel, they decided to go to the dinner. Alma showed absolutely no signs of worries and acted as if everything was normal. She was a very strong woman. The next day, Alma checked into UCLA hospital and had a hysterectomy. The day of the operation, Daddy went to eat in a restaurant near the hospital. Alma would say the restaurant became indelibly associated with a night of waiting in fear, and my father never returned to it afterward. Ever.

After immediate surgery and post-operative radiation, Mama recovered completely but was in the hospital for almost three weeks. Although Alma was out of danger, Hitch remained a complete wreck and continued to believe she was going to die. Unfortunately, she was unable to attend the opening of *Vertigo* in San Francisco, so I accompanied my father. After the showing there was a party, but Hitch, still in a depressed state, declined and I took him to his room. He just broke down in tears and said that he couldn't live without her and that he might as well jump out the window. Taking a rather large gamble, I told him that he was no good to her as he was, and pointed to the window. I left the room and returned to the party, hoping I didn't make a mistake. However, ten minutes later, I returned to the room and he was fast asleep. I really do feel that, had anything happened to her, he probably couldn't have gone on.

∼◦

WE DID ENJOY some happy events that year, including Joan Harrison's marriage to writer Eric Ambler. The following year was business as usual, and filming started on yet another Hitchcock classic, *North by Northwest* (1959), with our good friend Cary Grant, Eva Marie Saint (another cool blonde), James Mason (as one of Daddy's most stylish villains), Martin Landau, Jessie Royce Landis, and Leo G. Carroll. The script was written by Ernest Lehman with whom Daddy had worked on an unrealized project called *The Wreck of the Mary Deare* (Michael Anderson would end up directing that one with Gary Cooper and Charlton Heston in 1959).

North by Northwest was your typical Hitchcock story about a wrong man on the run trying to prove his innocence. What was amazing about the film was that, in addition to the colorful dialogue and crafty plot, it had amazing cinematic moments that set new standards. Like the crop dusting sequence with the plane chasing Cary Grant, or the climax on top of Mount Rushmore. Down to the last frame of the film (a train entering a tunnel as Cary Grant and Eva Marie Saint are embracing), the movie was perfect. I remember taking my daughters to visit the set. The crew was eager to please, and I remember Mary and Tere getting behind the camera. The film was an enormous success and we were all thrilled. Shortly after its release, Kathleen, my third daughter, was born. Alma and Hitch were both in good health again and they even got two new dogs: Geoffrey and Stanley. Life was going well, and it was about to get better.

1959–1969

*M*Y MOTHER WAS the first one to admit that Daddy's movies did not scare her. She was so familiar with the stories and followed the development of the scripts so closely, that by the time she saw the films, she knew what to expect. It was a whole different story for the audience, especially when it came to *Psycho* (1960). *Psycho* was first a brilliant novel by Robert Bloch. But when Daddy decided to make it his next picture, it changed film history. *Psycho* begins with Marion Crane (Janet Leigh), a secretary for a small real estate agency, who decides to steal a large amount of cash and join her lover, Sam Loomis (John Gavin), in the small town of Fairvale. She quickly realizes she made a mistake and plans on returning home, but heavy rains force her to pull into the Bates Motel, where she meets Norman Bates (Anthony Perkins), who lives at the motel with his sick old mother. Later that night, Marion is brutally murdered by Mrs. Bates in the shower, and Norman covers up all traces of the crime. Later, Marion's sister Lila (Vera Miles) comes to Fairvale to see Sam; she found out about the stolen money and thinks Sam is hiding Marion. Private detective Arbogast (Martin Balsam) also thinks that Sam is somehow involved, but the truth is, nobody knows what happened to Marion. Arbogast starts investigating the local motels, and when he meets Norman Bates, he begins to suspect that the young man or his mother may know something about Marion. He sneaks into the house behind the motel and is also stabbed to death by the mad old woman. When they get no news from the detective, Sam and Lila decide to go pay a visit to the Bates Motel, where they discover the horrifying truth. It turns out that Norman Bates killed his mother years ago and kept her body. Unable to deal with the guilt, he impersonated her and, at times, turned murderous.

The novel was slightly different from the film (in the book Norman Bates was short, overweight, and bald) but it was just as shocking. None of us, not even Mama, had any idea how groundbreaking the film would be. For one thing, it was done with Daddy's television crew. In other words, it was a low-budget film, not a glamorous picture—this time, no VistaVision, no beautiful costumes. The film was shot in black and white, and Herb Steinberg, who was the head of publicity at Paramount, suggested that it was probably Alma who, realizing that the film would be very violent, told Hitch that he might be able to get away with it if he did not shoot the film in color. Another controversial element was the fact that the film's star (my dear friend Janet Leigh) was killed within the first half-hour of the picture. Most actors are remembered for their grand entrances into a film; in this case, Ms. Leigh's death sequence in the shower is the most memorable scene of the movie. Anthony Perkins was also brilliant as the ambiguous and disturbed Norman Bates. Playing Norman would be both a blessing and a curse, as it would be difficult for him to get any other type of role later on in his career. He would be forever identified with Norman Bates.

The film was extremely daring for the time; it had a sexy opening (Janet Leigh and John Gavin, half-dressed in a romantic interlude), it was violent (the stabbing in the shower was made of many little pieces of film giving the impression that the knife did enter Janet's body), a few jolts (the murder of Martin Balsam), and a shocking revelation (Norman is his mother, and her decayed body is hidden in the fruit cellar). Today, everyone knows that Norman Bates *was* his mother and, therefore, the killer, but in 1960, that was a well-kept secret. Even audiences rushing to see the film, in a revolutionary publicity device, were asked not to reveal the ending. And no one was admitted into the theater once the movie started. The reviews were spectacular, the box office worldwide was phenomenal. But I have to be honest—when we made the film, we never thought we were making film history. But of course, when Daddy asked me to play a small part in the film, I immediately said yes. I played Caroline, who works with Marion Crane in the real estate office. I was—once again—the comic relief at the beginning of the film. Obviously, *Psycho* is very dark, so Daddy and screenwriter Joseph Stefano wanted to insert a bit of levity in that sequence. For instance, a man comes in with our boss, carrying a large amount in cash; he flirts with Marion. I only had a few lines in that sequence, but most of them related to my character's mother. Marion has a headache, and I suggest tranquilizers: "My mother's doctor gave them to me the day of my wedding. Teddy was furious when he found out I'd taken tranquilizers!" Marion: "Any phone calls?"

Caroline: "Teddy called me—my mother called to see if Teddy called. . . ." etc.

I'm not surprised that *Psycho* has been the center of many film studies; on a cinematic level, it is flawless, and it is also fascinating on a psychological level. Of all of my father's pictures, *Psycho* is the one that is most often cited, and part of the success has to be attributed to screenwriter Joseph Stefano. "After we had been talking for about a week and a half," Stefano recalled, "Hitch said that he and his wife Alma were going to take a cruise. And he said while I'm gone why don't you write the opening scene that takes place in the hotel room. I wrote it and gave it to him. And when he came back he said, 'Alma loved it.' I was very touched, because obviously, he liked it, too. He was a sentimental man, but he wouldn't show it. I had a very nice relationship with Hitchcock and Mrs. Hitchcock. She was just one of the nicest people I ever met in my life. She came in one day to his office to show him a toy she had found for their grandchild. I raved about it, and the next day there was one for my little boy. That's the way she was, very dear, very caring."

Peggy Robertson was Hitch's assistant on *Psycho*. They had met on the set of *Under Capricorn* (she was the continuity person on the film), and she became a regular on his films after *Vertigo*. Her duties on Hitch's films went beyond just assisting him. She would also do research for Daddy. She had actually been the one to point out that the novel *Psycho* by Robert Bloch had received very good reviews. She spent a lot of time with Alma, discussing projects and Hitch's work. She knew that in order to fully understand and work with Hitch, one had to also get close to Alma. Peggy passed away a few years ago, but she always had very fond memories of my mother: "Hitch's wife, Alma Reville, was the most important person to him in anything," she once said. "She was very brilliant. She had a very good brain, and her opinion was the most important opinion to him. Whatever we had—a

Peggy Robertson and Mama in the garden at our Santa Cruz home.

subject, a writer, an actor—'What did Alma think?' If Alma approved, we could go on. She was very vital. They worked together like the two halves of an orange. God sat on top of a mountain cutting up thousands of oranges and rolled them down the mountain. And occasionally the two right halves would meet and become a whole. That was the perfect one. That was Hitch and Alma. She was so good, so more than helpful to him, a partner to him. She had an extraordinary eye, she would point out things that other people had not noticed. Her word was absolute command."

My father would never ship a picture before he showed it to my mother. *Psycho* was completed, and Daddy ran it for Mama. At the end, she said, "It's great, but you can't ship the picture yet." "Why not?" Daddy asked, trying to figure out what was wrong with it. And she replied, "Because when Janet Leigh is lying dead on the bathroom floor after she has been stabbed, you can see her swallow!" Now, imagine all the hands this picture had passed through—the editor, the assistant editors, the sound editors, everyone who had seen the picture over and over—and no one had noticed it but Alma. So a few frames had to be taken out, and that's why in the final version, we cut from Janet Leigh lying on the bathroom floor to the shower head and then back to Janet Leigh. Initially, it had been designed as just one shot. This story is very indicative of Mama's knowledge of film. She was extraordinary, and Daddy trusted only her instincts.

~

THE UPCOMING RELEASE of *Psycho* and the success of the television series were a perfect excuse for Alma and Hitch to travel around the world—and to dine at the most amazing restaurants in the process! That year I recall Daddy became Chevalier du Tastevin in Dijon, France—a prestigious order acknowledging him as wine expert.

I found my parents' itinerary around the globe followed by their schedule prior to the release of *Psycho* and I was amazed by their heavy schedule:

April 3: 4 P.M. Leaving LA via APL *President Cleveland* for Honolulu—arrive in Honolulu on Friday, April 8, in the morning. Leave for Yokohama at 10 P.M. that day. At sea through Sunday, April 17, arrive in Yokohama, and motor to Tokyo. Arrive in Tokyo on Monday, April 18, staying at the Imperial Hotel. Leave Tokyo on Sunday, April 24, at 10 A.M. via BOAC Comet Jet Flight #965, to Hong Kong, arrival at 3 P.M. Staying at the Peninsula Hotel. Leave Hong Kong on Wednesday, April 27, at 11 A.M. via BOAC Comet Jet #961, arrive in Singapore at 1:20 P.M. same day, stay at

Raffles Hotel. Leave Singapore in the evening for Sydney on Tuesday, May 3, on BOAC #708. Arrive on Wednesday, May 4, in Sydney, staying at the Australia Hotel. Leave Sydney on Sunday, May 15, via Qantas Boeing 707 #571 at 1 P.M., arrive in Rome on Monday May 16 at 10:30 A.M. in Rome, stay at the Excelsior Hotel. On Tuesday, May 17, in the evening, travel to Ischia, staying at the Regina Isabella Hotel. Back in Rome on Sunday, May 22, stay at the Excelsior Hotel. Leave Rome for Paris on Thursday, May 26, on Air France Caravelle #633, arrival in Paris at noon, stay at the Plaza Athenée. Leaving for London on Tuesday, May 31, at 10 P.M., arrival at 11 P.M., stay at the Claridge's Hotel. Leaving for New York on Wednesday, June 8, Alma and Hitch return to LA on Monday, June 13.

Thursday, June 23, 4 P.M. *Psycho* was shown to the censors.

Monday, June 27, 2:30 P.M., they saw François Truffaut's *The 400 Blows*.

Tuesday, June 28, 2:30 P.M., they watched Billy Wilder's *The Apartment*.

Thursday, July 7, 3 P.M., screening of Ralph Thomas' *Conspiracy of Hearts.*

My parents spent a week in Japan for both business and to take in some sights. Daddy wanted to take a stroll along the Ginza and to see Mt. Fuji. They had first visited Japan in 1957, so this second visit was intended to revive showings of Daddy's *Alfred Hitchcock Presents* television series and to announce one-hour shows soon to arrive to Japan. Alma and Hitch took a tour of a film color studio lab and visited Singapore. They went back to Los Angeles for a few days, and then they were off to Australia. The press was constantly following my parents, and several women's magazines even did features on my mother. When talking to Alma, journalists were naturally curious about

her background, but they always inquired about Hitch. People were often amazed at how calm he looked; Alma would always mention the fact that Hitch never lost his temper, he never raised his voice on or off the set. She was also very modest and would repeatedly describe herself as a "homebody." She always underplayed her role in Hitch's movies. She kept it private.

Traveling around the world gave my parents an opportunity to meet all kinds of people and to embrace different cultures. They also got to socialize with some of their peers. For instance, arriving in Sydney at the same time as my parents was Charlton Heston, who was traveling for the premieres of *Ben-Hur* (1959) in Sydney and Melbourne. It was always fun to cross paths with other celebrities. It served as a little reminder that they would be heading back home soon to work on the next film.

FINDING THE NEXT project was always a challenge, but after *Psycho,* it became almost impossible. How do you follow up one of the best films of all time? Daddy wanted something different and challenging, and a short story by Daphne du Maurier called "The Birds" (1963) seemed complicated enough to pique his interest. Screenwriter Evan Hunter was brought in to flesh out the story and characters, and to move the setting from Cornwall to Bodega Bay (an area north of San Francisco). He did a masterful job. The short story had initially been bought for the television series, but after Daddy read of real bird attacks taking place, he felt that perhaps it could be made for the big screen. He had originally envisioned some apocalyptic plot but decided to focus on a small group of people (basically, a man, his mother, two women in love with him, and his sister) facing violent bird attacks. Evan Hunter lived in New York and had to move with his wife to California to collaborate on the script. The big test was, of course, dinner at my parents' house and meeting Alma. "I recall Alma was a tiny woman," Hunter said. "She was almost birdlike." Alma loved the Hunters and Hitch did, too. The collaboration was extremely productive. The short story is somewhat one-dimensional and, as customary in all Hitchcock pictures, the characters needed depth. There was a clinging mother played by our good friend Jessica Tandy (wife of Hume Cronyn); the son was Rod Taylor; the daughter, Veronica Cartwright; the son's ex-girlfriend was played by Suzanne Pleshette; and the love interest—the woman who comes to the small town looking for Rod Taylor after she briefly met him in a bird store—was played by a newcomer, Tippi Hedren. After Daddy and Evan agreed on the plot and the characters, Evan began writing—and Hitch would check up on him daily, by innocently calling Evan's wife. He never came right out and asked how the script was going, but he was subtlely making sure that Evan was indeed at the typewriter.

During the writing of the script, on November 6, 1961, to be precise, there was a terrible fire in Bel Air that destroyed several homes. I tried to get in touch with my parents (my husband, my daughters, and I were living in the Valley), but the phone just kept ringing. I panicked and decided to drive over there with Peggy Robertson, Daddy's assistant. We got to the house and rang the bell, but there was no electricity so I finally had to use my spare key. We found my parents peacefully asleep. It turned out that Daddy had spent the day hosing down the roof and the surrounding area of the house. That way, he thought, the fire would be stopped. Feeling safe, Hitch and Alma simply went to bed.

~⌒

HITCH AND ALMA knew that, although *The Birds* would not only be the title but the stars of the film as well, the casting was a crucial aspect of the production. Now that Grace Kelly was Princess of Monaco, my parents wanted to find her a worthy successor—and they wanted an unknown actress, someone they could turn into a star. One morning, Daddy and Mama saw a commercial on television (during the *Today Show*) for a dietary product featuring a beautiful blonde—her name was Tippi Hedren. My father had his new agent at MCA, Herman Citron, contact the beautiful actress on his behalf. And thus began a series of screen tests. Edith Head would design the costumes (and come up with a personal wardrobe especially designed for Tippi), and Martin Balsam (Arbogast in *Psycho*) rehearsed with Tippi scenes from *Rebecca, Notorious,* and *To Catch a Thief.* Tippi would also come over to our house where my parents would both go over the scenes with her. Again, Alma had a great deal to do with a lot of the early work and had a very, very strong presence throughout the process. Eventually, Tippi did the screen tests; it was an extraordinary time. The tests were put together and everyone looked at them except for Tippi. Then Alma and Hitch invited Tippi to dinner at Chasen's, their favorite restaurant. At the table, Lew Wasserman was sitting to her left and my parents to her right. Daddy gave her a very beautifully wrapped package from Gump's, a jewelry store in San Francisco. It was one of his favorite shops. Tippi opened the box, and inside it was a beautiful pin of three birds in flight with pearls and gold. She looked over at Hitch and he said, "We want you to play the part of Melanie Daniels in *The Birds*." Tippi started to cry. Alma cried. Even Hitch and Lew had tears in their eyes. It was a very exciting evening. And then the work really began.

~

MAMA AND I went up to see Daddy in Bodega Bay in Northern California, where the exteriors were shot—the interiors and some of the most complicated action sequences were done at Universal Studios, where Daddy now had an office (headed by Peggy Robertson and personal secretary Suzanne Gautier). I remember we were visiting when they were shooting the bird attack at the birthday party. There was a trained seagull named Charlie, and they had wired his beak shut so he wouldn't hurt anyone. At lunchtime, Charlie decided to take a walk, and I remember the sudden panic on the set. They ran up and down the beach, looking for Charlie, who had to be back on time for his close-ups! Mama and I laughed so hard! Daddy was probably the only one who stayed calm. All kinds of birds were used in the film—even fake ones that were like hand puppets. There were many special visual effects used in the film—remember, computer-generated images did not exist then. Many birds had to be shot separately and were then added on top of some of the already existing scenes (like the one where the birds come down the chimney or the attack on Tippi in the attic). The collaboration of art director Robert Boyle, matte artist wizard Albert Whitlock, director of photography Robert Burks, and other experts made it all blend seamlessly. Alma and I visited the set quite frequently, and each time we went, they'd be trying something new. But it was hard to see what the final result would be, even in dailies, because the shots were incomplete since many elements were added later. Needless to say, when I first saw the

finished film, I could not believe my eyes. Daddy had also exper-
imented with sound design and decided to have sophisticated
bird sound effects in place of music. Composer Bernard
Herrmann stepped in to create a very elaborate soundtrack for
the film. Despite all of the innovative visual and sound techniques, I don't think the film received its due when it came out.
Alma would agree that everyone expected *Psycho* with birds. But
the film was a complete departure not only from *Psycho,* but
from anything else Daddy had previously attempted in his
career. *The Birds* was, in my eyes, a (successful) experiment, but
again it was ahead of its time and would take several years for it
to reach the cult status it deserved. The film was an event
nonetheless—a global event. Alma traveled all over the world
with Hitch and Tippi to promote the film. The most memorable
opening took place at the Cannes Film Festival in France, where
Hitch was, more than anywhere else in the world, acknowledged as a true artist, as a film auteur. His work was inspiring
young filmmakers of the New Wave, such as Claude Chabrol,
Eric Rohmer, and of course, François Truffaut, who would write
the most notable book ever done on my father's work. I am of
course biased: The book is dedicated to me. He wrote: "Alfred
Hitchcock made 53 films and one daughter. I dedicate this book
to Patricia Hitchcock O'Connell." Truffaut would become a
dear friend of ours and would make a very moving speech at the
American Film Institute Life Achievement Award ceremony celebrating Daddy's career in 1979.

～

ALMA AND HITCH had initially started working on *Marnie*
(1964) right after *Psycho.* Joseph Stefano, who had done an
incredible adaptation of the novel *Psycho* by Robert Bloch, then
wrote a story treatment based on a novel by Winston Graham.
Marnie was to star Grace Kelly, but because of her duties as
Princess of Monaco, she could not make the comeback to the

Tippi Hedren and my parents arriving in France for the opening of The Birds *at the Cannes Film Festival.*

screen as she had originally intended in *Marnie*. In response to Grace turning down the project, Hitch wrote her the following letter, dated June 26, 1962:

> Dear Grace,
>
> Yes, it is sad, wasn't it. I was looking forward so much to the fun and pleasure of our doing a picture again. Without a doubt, I think you made, not only the best decision, but the only decision, to put the project aside at this time.
>
> After all, it was only a movie. Alma joins me in sending our most fondest and affectionate thoughts for you.
>
> Hitch
>
> PS: I have enclosed a small tape recording which I made especially for [Prince] Rainer. Please ask him to play it privately. It is not for all ears.

I NEVER KNEW what was on that tape—but I can only imagine! When *Marnie* was revived after Daddy did *The Birds*, Tippi was the logical choice for the lead, and because Joseph Stefano was now busy on another project, Daddy turned to Evan Hunter to adapt the book. Their collaboration on this project was short-lived, however, as they disagreed on a particular scene—the so-called rape scene in which the central male figure of the story forces himself on his frigid wife. Jay Presson Allen (famous at the time for *The Prime of Miss Jean Brodie,* an extraordinary play and a film in 1969 for which Jay would receive an Academy Award nomination) was brought in to work on the script. She and her husband, producer Lewis M. Allen, instantly became very close to my parents.

At the center of the story of *Marnie* is a very troubled and complex woman who is a compulsive thief and is pursued by a man obsessed with unlocking her fears and her secrets—we find out that when she was just a little girl she killed a sailor whom she thought was abusing her mother. *Marnie* was attractive to Hitch in that it was very different from *The Birds*. Yet it tied in with themes he had explored in many of his films. And Jay Presson Allen (who would later write *Cabaret, Prince of the City, Deathtrap, Lord of the Flies,* and others) made an enormous contribution to this intricate and complicated psychological thriller. Jay Presson Allen has many wonderful memories of my parents and shared them with me for this book:

"Hitch loved to work with women," Jay explained. "He felt that with women, he didn't have to waste any energy on control. And he liked women; he surrounded himself with women. He loved his wife, his daughter, and his home. The minute that it appeared perfectly clear that we were going to get along, he brought me to his home. And I worked as much in and out of Hitch's house as I did anywhere else. I stayed there for a while as well. My first impression of Alma was that she was extremely bright. Small. Quick. Very quick. Not a spark of glamour, very plain. But you liked to look at her because she was so receptive and so open and so fast. You know she read you immediately, and that was extremely attractive to me. Alma was warm. Hitch was warm but only when he wanted to be. She was a good conversationalist, and as I got to know her better, we found that we had the same hatreds, and that we loathed the same people (particularly certain people in Hitch's professional life that she and I simply could not stand). Hitch was more diplomatic and could hide his disdain by pulling pranks on them. Alma was discreet about it all while being very opinionated. She was the one with the common sense; she was real; she read people. And Hitch depended on her because he was more fantastical, he needed her to ground him.

"Alma was fantastic in the kitchen—there was a cook (who had studied her craft in France), but Alma did most of the cooking. And Alma's cooking was very simple but delicious. There

was a huge walk-in freezer in their kitchen. They flew in fish and meat weekly directly from England. Incidentally, Hitch and I shared a complete hatred for eggs. But no matter what, Hitch did the washup. One night, I sat there, watching him cleanup and I said, 'I can help if you'd like.' He replied, 'No. Thank you, but I can manage on my own.' I sat through several evenings of that routine and finally I said, 'Look, I'm as good as you are with washing dishes.' He replied, 'Please let me see what you can do.' So he sat back and watched me do the cleanup. When I was finished, he said, 'Perfect, now we can do business!'

"And that's really how I started working with him on *Marnie*. I know for a fact that Alma did a lot of work on the scripts—but when you were working with Hitch, there was never a hint of the collaboration. It was very discreet and strictly between them. I never saw the story notes she wrote on my drafts of *Marnie*, but I knew certain comments were coming from her. We did socialize a bit but not much. When we did, she was extremely good company; she was not the type to sit back like a little mouse. Always affable, she would make interesting comments about everything. She was a film buff and had strong opinions about movies. I remember she liked *The Birds* a lot.

"She and Hitch came to New York about twice a year, and they saw all the big plays; they loved the theater. When they were in town, we were always invited to join them at parties; and I think Alma was responsible for that. Alma loved my husband, Lewis, and treated him almost like a son. But both Hitch and Alma took us in as if we were family. I remember Hitch would say he wanted to get a yacht, so that we could go around the world with he and Alma. The idea was that we would be working on the screen adaptation of *Three Hostages,* one of the book sequels to *The 39 Steps* written by John Buchan. It was going to be a two-year trip. But it never came to pass. My husband and I were also invited by the Hitchcocks to their ranch in Santa Cruz. I remember we spent a fourth of July weekend up there with them. My husband Lewis is, like Hitch was, a lover of good wine. So every day we were at the ranch, before lunch, Hitch would take Lewis in the library and would open a bottle of Blanc de Blanc—and they would drink the whole bottle together. Lewis was plastered for four days. Hitch also would take him to his wine cellar where he kept some amazing vintage bottles. One of them was the last of six bottles left in the world—and it was served at our table one night.

"Santa Cruz was so pretty and so easy and so comfortable. The interesting thing was that in Santa Cruz or in Bel Air, there was never the feeling of anything grand. Both Alma and Hitch kept it all very simple.

"To my recollection, although she was opinionated and contributed a great deal to any conversation, Alma never talked about the past. And she never pushed herself forward. The only ego she displayed was in her presence—she was really *there,* she did not disappear. Hitch and Alma loved to relax. That's why we got along so well. I remember we read a lot when we were with them. Writing *Marnie* was a great experience, although I must admit that, unfortunately, I am not crazy about the film. I don't think it really works. The audience did not respond to the film at all.

"After the film was completed, we stayed close and saw each other a lot. I did write another script for Hitch, *Mary Rose*. He paid me himself because Universal did not believe in the project. And it was never made. We stayed friends even after that experience. When Lewis and I saw them, it was if we had never left. Both Alma and Hitch had a great sense of humor. He knew how to deliver a line, but she knew how to tell jokes. Alma made him endlessly comfortable; she made him comfortable as a man; she made him comfortable in the house, around other people, and in business."

∼

ALTHOUGH IT WAS pretty much kept between my parents, Mama was extremely involved in the development of the screenplay for *Marnie*. I found some of the notes she wrote on the different drafts. They're quite indicative of her story sense but also of the fact that she liked logic. Oftentimes, she would point out things that did not completely make sense. Other times, she would suggest changes to improve character development or make new suggestions for the plot.

The revised and final script of Marnie was delivered on October 9, 1963, and distributed on October 11, 1963. The distribution of the actual script for review read as follows:

1- Mrs. Hitchcock
2- Mr. Hitchcock
3- Peggy Robertson

Notice how my mother's name was placed first on the list.

Although it was dropped in the end, there was a sequence with Marnie working as an usherette in a movie theater. In her notes, Alma felt that the description was not detailed enough and indicated, "We should put in the words that Marnie is dressed in the uniform of a cinema usherette."

Alma objected to some dialogue between Mark (the lead character played by Sean Connery) and Lil (his sister in law played by Diane Baker) at his wedding ceremony and suggested that sequence be shortened. In the end, it was completely deleted from the script.

Mama also noticed inconsistencies such as, "In one scene, the script indicates Marnie locks a door. In the next scene, her husband *comes through the door.* How did he unlock the door?"

Alma continued making notes and comments during production as she was invited by Daddy on occasions to watch dailies. The following notes have to do with her concern about certain lines of dialogue:

1—Scene 144—Interior Ward's Outside Office: Can we lose Susan's line: "You ever notice how in the movies it's always the cool, ladylike type who turns out to be the sex-pot?"

2—Scene 239—Interior Ward's Outer Office prior to washroom scene, add background dialogue (off-screen)
"Good night!"
"Have a nice weekend!"
"See you Monday!"
These off-screen lines should be added at the beginning of the scene.

3—Scene 266 [In that scene, Marnie is robbing the company safe and realizes that the cleaning lady is there. She takes off her shoes, puts them in her pocket, and starts walking out . . . but one shoe falls to the ground. The cleaning woman doesn't react: She is hard of hearing! Marnie rushes out as the night watchman walks into frame. Mama was concerned about this scene being clear to the audience]:

The watchman's lines: "You're sure making time tonight, Rita. What's the big rush?" should be brought way up in dubbing so that it is absolutely clear that the cleaning woman (Rita) is hard of hearing. Maybe we should redub Rita's line, "I wanta get to bed, that's what's the big rush," in a more hushed voice.

4—Scene 277—Interior Howard Johnson's Restaurant: Redub Marnie's line, where it sounds as though she says "Cold."

5—Scene 288—Exterior Wykwyn—departure for honeymoon. The cut of the car departing should come later. We should have a close-up of Lil, then cut to the departing car, then back to a close-up of Lil.

6—Scene 310—Interior ship's cabin: Redub for clarity Mark's line: "Now why don't we try to get some rest? How about it? You *way* over here in your bed . . . and me *light years* away over there in mine?"

7—Scenes 358–359—Interior Wykwyn Hall: We should see Lil go to the library door and listen. Play the sound of Marnie dialing on the telephone over Lil leaving the library door before she goes upstairs.

8—Scene 403—Interior stables: Rewrite Lil's line: "And I mean to have him. This business with you, whatever it is . . . this little intermission . . . when the curtain goes up on the last act . . . the leading lady, *c'est moi.* Dig?" so that there is not so much of the theater in the dialogue. [This scene was deleted from the film.]

9—Scene 404—Redub Marnie's line: "Mazel tov, dear" so that she says, "Morning, dear."

SCENES WERE ALWAYS shot several times, but not all of them are printed and viewed at dailies. At least two or three takes, sometimes more, were selected, viewed, and one was finally chosen for the film. Again, during that process, my mother had the opportunity to voice her suggestions on at least one occasion on record:

1—Scene 314: Interior Ship's Cabin: Prefer the shot of Mark smoking in bed—pan to Marnie seated on couch in sitting room. Prefer the take of Marnie leaning over on the couch rather than the take of her sitting upright.

2—Scene 322: Interior Ship's Cabin: Prefer the straight-on shot of Mark seated rather than the angle shooting down.

3—Scene 333D: Interior Ship's Cabin: Prefer that Marnie's head does not turn away on the bed. It does not look as though Marnie lays on the bed.

ALTHOUGH *MARNIE* WAS not the success Hitch and Alma had originally hoped for, the film has gotten better with age. Tippi Hedren and Sean Connery were perfectly matched. The supporting cast included Louise Latham as Marnie's domineering mother and Diane Baker as Marnie's rival, and they were both equally brilliant. "I met Alma and Hitch together," Diane Baker recalled. "I've always thought of her as a very quiet, darling person who was totally committed to her husband. She seemed to be there for him in every aspect of his life. And she was very much there at the forefront when I first visited them at their home. I remember Alma was making quiche, and we just sat in the kitchen. And one point, she brought in a magazine with a picture of Grace Kelly and pointed out the resemblance they felt I had to her. I think that's one of the reasons why I got the part."

Beyond the brilliant acting in the film, *Marnie* should also be treasured, as it marked the end of an era in my father's career.

This was the last film he did with his director of photography Robert Burks and his editor George Tomasini. They both passed away shortly after completing the movie. Without a doubt, their contributions to Daddy's movies (Mr. Burks did thirteen films with my father and Mr. Tomasini, twelve) were an integral part of the movies' success. Equally as important was the music, which in *Marnie,* is often quoted as Bernard Herrmann's best. Mr. Herrmann would follow *Marnie* with *Torn Curtain* (1966), but unfortunately, he and my father had a difference of opinion. Bernard Herrmann was replaced by another composer (John Addison) and, thus, ended their association.

~

I REMEMBER MAMA telling me a funny story that happened during the making of *Marnie* that is very indicative of how well she understood Hitch and how protective she could be of him. One evening, Hitch came home from the studio in an extremely bad mood. "What's wrong, is the leading lady getting out of hand?" Alma asked him.

"Oh, nothing like that," he said. "It's just that there's something mysterious going on at the studio, and I haven't been able to put my finger on it. I think some of the people are keeping a little secret from me."

Alma made a few discreet inquiries and discovered that the "little secret" was simply a plan by some members of Hitch's production company to throw a surprise party for him. Alma put a stop to the plan immediately. It was a charming and thoughful idea, but the results would have been catastrophic. Hitch simply hated surprises—unless he was the instigator.

A side note: *Marnie* was produced for Universal by my father's production company "Geoffrey Stanley," named after my parents' two dogs. Both dogs appeared with Daddy in his cameo in *The Birds.*

My parents were not exactly big on birthdays. We would celebrate them, but because there were only three of us, it was always very simple. It became a bigger deal later on after my daughters were born, and Hitch and Alma would give catered parties in the backyard of their house in Bel Air.

Yet my parents never forgot their friends' birthdays. They would have flowers (I remember Azalea plants, Anthurium, red roses and/or wine) delivered to the special people in their life. They gave specific instructions to Bekins Van & Storage, where some of their vintage wine was kept, and would, for instance, give instructions to deliver Chateau Haut Brion 1961 in magnums numbers 192, 193, or 194 to their driver, Tony Emerzian.

My parents celebrating their 73rd birthdays on the set of Frenzy *in 1972.*

Likewise, their friends never forgot their birthdays, especially given that they were born only one day apart. Alma and Hitch loved receiving gifts—they were always grateful and would immediately write a note back: "Alma [or sometimes, Daddy would write Madame—French for "Mrs."] and I send our warmest appreciation of your most welcome birthday remembrance, and thank you very much indeed." One of their own personal favorite cards was one I sent to them: "You may have thought no one knew when your birthday was . . . but it leaked out! [The card showed a little boy on a potty.] Happy birthday, love Pat!"

Alma and Hitch were very generous with my daughters. Alma spent a lot of time with them. They adored her, and occasionally, feared her. "One afternoon, Grandma had come home from a trip," Mary remembered. "We all met at the house. After a short while, I sneaked some cigarettes into the guest bathroom and tried lighting them. Because I didn't know what I was doing, I proceeded to set the roll of toilet paper on fire. My parents pretty much knew I was the culprit even though I hotly denied it. By the time we got home, I was in a lot of trouble. My parents gave me the worst possible punishment—I had to call my grandmother and admit what I had done. I cared so much about what she thought of me that I was absolutely petrified. She was very sweet and accepting of my apology, which made me feel even worse. I was so worried that she would think differently of me but she never did.

"During my adolescence, my skin was the typical teenage complexion. My grandmother would take me with her to Elizabeth Arden Salons for facials. She said 'they would clear up my spots on my American skin.' I'd come out looking worse than when I went in! But it meant a lot that she wanted to help me!"

At the same time, Mama was a true friend to my daughters: "She had some of my grandfather's playful humor," Katie remembers. "One example was that when I was only four and in pre-school, she gave me a finger painting set, so I did a painting for her, just a mix of splotches and blotches. She liked it so much, or so she said, that she had it specially framed in a beautiful gold frame and hung it in the entryway of their home for all to see. Because my grandparents were collectors of fine art, their friends who saw my painting assumed that it was done by some well-known artist. They would ask my grandmother who the Impressionist was who painted it and would offer their interpretation on the use of color and lighting. My grandmother would listen intently and then would merely reply that it was done by a 'fine young artist' whose identity she could not disclose."

~o~

MY PARENTS WERE not political, but looking back at my mother's collection of photo albums, I found correspondence with three American presidents. The first one came from President John F. Kennedy; it was an invitation: "The President requests your company at luncheon on Tuesday December 10th, 1963, at 1 P.M." The invitation was postmarked November 21, 1963. President Kennedy was shot the next day. In 1965, Lew Wasserman asked Daddy to be the host of the inaugural ball luncheon after Johnson was elected President. Imagine the excitement for both my parents! It was a great honor and Alma was so proud when Hitch walked to the stage and hosted a portion of the evening. Here is, published for the first time, my father's speech:

Washington, D.C. Inaugural Gala, Monday, January 18, 1965:

"Mr. President, Mrs. Johnson, Mr. Vice President–elect, Mrs. Humphrey–elect, ladies, and gentlemen: [Daddy did his usual bow] Good evening. I am very pleased to be part of this salute to a great man. It is an honor I shall always cherish. There is a reason why this is especially moving for me. You probably don't realize this, but I am not a native-born American. I migrated to these shores twenty-five years ago. Some people say it was a kind of cultural exchange . . . but no one knows what was sent to England in return. They're afraid to open it.

"Actually, that is not the case at all. The year I came to the United States a young congressman from Texas voted for a bill called 'Lend-Lease.' Now he can see what he got for those fifty destroyers. Actually, I suspect that our producer, Mr. Richard Adler, chose me to open this show because of my reputation as a political prognosticator. The identity of our first family is hardly a surprise to me. A few years ago I warned the entire nation: '*The Birds* is coming!'

"In two days, this great country will pause and turn to Washington for the occasion of the forty-fifth inauguration of a President of the United States. That day will demand and receive all the solemn dignity that the office and the man assuming it have earned. But tonight we are asking you to relax and enjoy yourselves. I am certain that none of you will be more relaxed than our Vice President–elect. Mr. Humphrey is in what we call 'the awkward age.' No longer a senator; not yet a vice president.

"Mr. Adler has assembled a formidable group of entertainers for tonight's show. Many of you in our audience, as members of the administration, or of the House, or Senate, have worked for the minimum wage. Tonight it is our turn. This unique country has selected a theme for the next four years—the Great Society. A theme has also been selected for this evening's event—the free expression of the human spirit, without which, no Great Society could be possible. To demonstrate that theme, we have one of Broadway and television's brightest choreographers, Mr. Ernie Flatt, assisted by a handsome troop of

Broadway performers, including Buzz Miller, George Reader, and Don Crichton.

[Later, after the performance:]

"Thank you. I thought they did quite well without me. Originally, of course, I was to have danced with them. After all, I understand that is the way the junior senator from California got started. Unfortunately for me, at the last moment, someone stole my leotard.

"Our next performer is a young singer who is closely associated with the number that was selected only last week as the official song of the Army Reservists in honor of their Secretary of Defense: 'Mack the Knife.' Ladies and gentlemen: Mr. Bobbie Darrin.

[After the performance:]

"Thank you. We shall continue our program in a moment, but first . . . a word from our sponsor. The party or parties to whom this is directed do not seem to be very well represented here tonight. In fact, they aren't even well represented in Congress. This is addressed to our loyal opposition.

"Friends:

"On last November 4th did you suffer from that morning-after feeling? Did you feel as though your group had all the cavities?

"Are you hurt because no one put you in the driver's seat?

"Do you want fast, fast, fast relief; yet, you'd rather fight than switch?

"Then the answer is indeed a simple one: You're number two, so you'll just have to try harder.

"And now, an international visitor. We next have an extraordinary young man who has flown here all the way from Paris where he is in the process of making a motion picture, the producers of which have generously suspended operations until his return. *Messieurs et mesdames, avec beaucoup de plaisir, je vous presente Monsieur Woody Allen.* [Ladies and gentlemen, it gives me great pleasure to introduce Mr. Woody Allen.]

[Later, after Woody Allen's speech:]

"Thank you. You know this has all been most enlightening. I always thought Woody Allen was a national park.

"I don't believe it is commonly known but my great-great-grandfather once had dinner at the White House. Actually, it wasn't exactly dinner. It was during the War of 1812 and was more in the nature of a barbecue. At the time the hostess was Dolly Madison. I have come to the end of my part in these festivities but it is with a great deal of pleasure that I turn you over to another Dolly. Ladies and gentlemen, Miss Carol Channing."

Daddy returned to his table, waving at a few people. Alma was smiling, and anxious to start the meal. On the menu:

DELICES OF MARYLAND WITH PAUL MASSON EMERALD DRY
ROCK CORNISH GAME HEN
STRINGBEANS STROGANNOFF
BRAISED ENDIVES WITH INGLENOOK CABERNET SAUVIGNON
FIESTA SALAD
TRAPPIST CHEESE
BAVAROIS SATO, PETITS FOURS SECS
ALAMADEN BLANC DE BLANC, 1959

THE NEXT DAY, a newspaper story appeared featuring a gorgeous picture of Hitch, wearing a suit and bow tie, and Alma, exquisitely dressed in a beautiful gown and bolero created by Edith Head: "There was no mystery about this gentleman when he arrived to dine at the White House. Even the most amateur gumshoes knew that he was Alfred (suspense) Hitchcock. With him is Mrs. Hitchcock looking not a bit worried."

∼

IN MY MOTHER'S scrapbooks and photo albums, I also found letters from Pat Nixon and an invitation to the White House from President Ford. But the best one was from Senator John Glenn, personally addressed just to Alma and dated July 28, 1975.

Dear Alma:
    Certainly enjoyed meeting you at Lew Wasserman's luncheon last Saturday. That was quite an affair. If you're ever in the Washington, D.C. area, please drop by my office. Best regards and look forward to seeing you again.
                                                    Sincerely, John Glenn.

∼

WHILE DADDY CONTINUED to rely on Mama to help him pick his next project, he was also at a crossroad in his career. The studios were changing, and young filmmakers were creating a whole new style of cinema. With the failure of *Marnie,* my father thought he should do something closer in scope to some of his bigger pictures, like *North by Northwest.* Hitch got the idea for his next movie, *Torn Curtain* (1966), when he heard of the true story of two British diplomats, Guy Burgess and Donald Maclean, who had defected to Russia. Hitch wondered, "What did Mrs. Maclean think of the whole thing?" The film centers on a scientist who pretends to be defecting to Russia, and has to lie even to his girlfriend, while he is in reality spying for the Americans and planning on stealing a secret formula. Novelist Brian Moore was hired to write the script. Later on, British writers Keith Waterhouse and Willis Hall did a dialogue polish, but an arbitration with the Writers Guild determined that their contribution did not justify screen credit. Paul Newman and

Torn Curtain was Daddy's 50th movie.

Julie Andrews were cast in the lead roles, and Daddy had to rush into production to accommodate Julie's schedule—before he was completely satisfied with the script. *Torn Curtain* has some great moments; one of them is a murder scene involving Paul Newman trying to kill a man. The trick is he has to do it in complete silence (to avoid alerting a cab driver waiting for him outside the house), and he ends up dragging his victim on the floor and shoving his head inside a gas oven. "Murder can be fun," Hitch used to say. "People are killed so easily in films, nobody ever goes back to take a second look to see whether they're really dead or not. The whole idea was not only to show how difficult it is to kill a man, but to point up to the character what espionage entails: you're involved in killing!"

Torn Curtain was no *North by Northwest* but, while it was never featured as one of my parents' favorites, it definitely emerged as a legitimate Hitchcock picture. Daddy used to tell us that he felt satisfied if he got 75 percent of his original vision on the screen. With *Torn Curtain*, I think he had most certainly accomplished his ambition.

∼

IT WOULD BE three years before Hitch could find another project. In the intervening time, the book *Hitchcock/Truffaut* was published, and Hitch would develop several projects (including one called *Kaleidoscope*). Daddy would also receive (on April 10, 1968) the Irving Thalberg Award from the Academy of Motion Picture Arts and Sciences. "Always a bridesmaid, never a bride," Hitch once said about the fact that he never got an Academy Award for his work. When the Thalberg Award was handed out to him by his friend Lew Wasserman, Daddy simply said "Thank you." Other accolades would follow, including the DW Griffith Award from the Directors Guild of America and the French Legion of Honor, but Hitch would never receive an Oscar. Hitch was nominated several times: once in the best film category as producer for *Suspicion,* and as best director for *Lifeboat, Spellbound, Rear Window,* and *Psycho.* My mother stood proudly next to Daddy on all those occasions.

∼

ALMA KNEW THAT Hitch had to keep busy. She could not imagine him *not* working on a project. There was never any doubt that Hitch should keep on working, and Alma was pleased when he finally got busy on his next film, *Topaz* (1969), based on the novel by Leon Uris. It was a complex thriller about the Cuban missile crisis and a romance between an American agent and a beautiful Cuban woman working for the underground against her own nation. Unfortunately, the film, which reunited Daddy with *Vertigo* screenwriter Samuel Taylor, was to become yet another unsuccessful film.

By the late sixties, films were being shot mainly on location, away from soundstages, but my father still liked the confinement of the studio (in *Topaz*, the streets of Harlem were recreated at Universal Studios). To the critics, his films were becoming old-fashioned or were not hip enough for a public that was racing to see either James Bond or, at the other end of the spectrum, films like *Blow-Up* (1966) that were breaking rules and creating a whole new way of telling stories. *Topaz*, like *Torn Curtain,* had some great moments, as well as an international cast (Frederick Stafford, John Forsythe, Michel Piccoli, Philippe Noiret, Claude Jade, and others), but audiences and critics simply did not get it. The sneak previews were disastrous, and several endings had to be filmed. Those were trying times for Daddy, and the only thing that kept him balanced were Mama and his family. Alma kept encouraging him and always remained positive, while making sure he was always comfortable at home. Perhaps Daddy needed a change—and new horizons. It turns out that returning to his roots in London to make his next film was exactly what the doctor prescribed.

Last Films. Last Days.

*M*Y MOTHER USED to say that *Frenzy* (1972) is the one movie where the Hitchcock touch came back. She was not suggesting that Hitch had necessarily lost his touch; she was referring to the type of material Hitch was dealing with. *Frenzy* had a very good (and twisted) story and marked a return to my father's best thrillers. I put it right up there with *Psycho*. The screenplay, written by Anthony Shaffer (*Sleuth*), was based on a novel by Arthur LaBern (titled *Goodbye Picadilly, Farewell Leicester Square*) and was about a man wrongly accused of strangling women. Despite the grim subject matter, the film also had a lot of humorous moments—including scenes between the detective on the case and his wife, who is not-too-successfully experimenting in the kitchen. *Frenzy* was not a glamorous picture. Daddy cast amazing talent, but they were mainly stage actors or names that were mostly recognizable in Europe (Jon Finch, Barry Foster, Anna Massey, Barbara Leigh-Hunt, Alec MacCowen, and Elsie Randolph in a small but memorable role). Part of the story took place in Covent Garden meat and vegetable market where Daddy grew up. During filming, an old man even came up to him and said he had known his father.

But while in London, the unexpected happened. Alma had given my daughter Mary a trip to Europe as a high school graduation present. Mary left Los Angeles on a plane bound for London. Upon arriving, there was no one to meet her until finally Hitch showed up. On the way to the Claridges hotel, he told Mary the reason for his lateness—Alma had suffered a stroke that morning. Mary became very worried. "I remember she kept apologizing for being ill. I was very frightened for her. That night, we all had dinner in the hotel room. I had to continuously help her and wipe her mouth," Mary remembers. "In such a short time, we had reversed roles. I was now taking care of her when I had been the one to rely on her. It was a tough adjustment." Daddy called me and said that the only thing Alma was worried about was Mary's trip and she wanted me to come to London and take her place as tour guide. I quickly packed and took off.

Alma wanted to stay at the Claridges and refused to go to the hospital. Although the stroke was serious, it wasn't life-threatening. Her speech was slightly affected, as were one arm and, to a lesser degree, one leg. Mama was not well, but her mind hadn't been touched and she was very pleased when I arrived. Naturally, Hitch was distraught but managed to finish the picture. Hazel Singer, sister of Daddy's assistant Peggy Robertson, remembers that painful time: "I sent some flowers to the hotel for Alma. The next morning, ill as she was, there was a note from her, written in a rather shaky hand, thanking me for them. This was typical of her exquisite manners and high standards."

Mary and I went on the trip that Alma had arranged. The hotels where we stayed had the most luxurious suites. Hitch had had his secretary make a travel guide, a tiny notebook with all kinds of special instructions for Alma, and thank God he did, or Mary and I would have been completely lost! The most amusing moment of the trip was when Mary and I were waiting to have an audience with the Pope at the Vatican in Rome. They called the name "Hitchcock," and one of the papal guards hummed the theme from the *Alfred Hitchcock Presents* television series (The Funeral March of the Marionette by Charles Gounot).

Mama returned to America as soon as she was well enough to travel and went into the hospital to be thoroughly checked; then she stayed with us until Daddy returned. I don't know of anyone who had such strength and greater willpower to recover. After she returned home, my mother had a physical therapist and worked so hard that she recovered from most of the side effects of the initial stroke. She became strong enough to go on the publicity tour for *Frenzy* with Hitch, and although it was tiring for her, she kept on going. Her presence at his side was very important to Daddy; *Frenzy* was acknowledged as an instant classic worldwide. Many were saying this was one of his best films.

Life at home seemed to be getting back to normal, and normal meant that Daddy was moving onto another project, *Family Plot*, based on the novel *The Rainbird Pattern* by British novelist Victor Canning. Hitch was attracted to the basic idea and enlisted his friend Ernest Lehman to adapt the book—but what they did was turn the drama into a bit of a comedy, while keeping the basic premise of two amateur cons (Bruce Dern and Barbara Harris) who get involved in a frightening case of kidnapping (orchestrated by Karen Black and William Devane).

～つ

ONE HIGHLIGHT IN 1974, as Hitch was preparing the film, was his being honored by the Film Society of Lincoln Center. Hitch had at his side Alma and Princess Grace. But both my parents' health were frail, and in October 1974, Daddy had to have a pacemaker. Mama stayed strong for the both of them, always calm and relaxed, because she wanted Daddy to keep concentrating on work. She did not want him to worry about her or about his own health. We visited them often, and one time, Hitch was determined to show us *Rebecca*. He got a 16mm projector and a print of the film but simply couldn't figure out how to make it work. Later, Lew Wasserman gave him one of the first Sony Betamax video machines. Daddy would stand by the machine while Mary read the instructions. They had given him a video copy of *Rear Window*. "I'd say, 'Press start,' but it simply didn't work," Mary remembers. Alma quietly stayed uninvolved as they tried to make it work. What surprises me is that both Hitch and Alma knew more about filmmaking than anyone— they had practically invented it—and yet they couldn't figure out how to work a VCR! I laugh when I think about it especially since I'm just as bad with new technologies today as they once were. One night, we watched *Casablanca* and Daddy just started crying when Ingrid Bergman came onscreen. "Wasn't she beautiful," he said. I'll never forget another evening when we all saw *Born Free*; we all sat in the kitchen afterward, speechless and crying our eyes out. If my father and mother had seen Steven Spielberg's *E.T. The Extra-Terrestrial*, I am convinced it would have been their favorite film ever. An interesting contrast to the type of films they made.

～

ON WEDNESDAY, AUGUST 13, 1974, Hitch turned 75—and Alma did, too, the next day. They celebrated at their favorite restaurant, Chasen's. Then, at last, *Family Plot* went into production. It was a difficult shoot; Hitch wasn't well most of the time, and he was extremely worried about Alma. He tried to maintain his good spirit and managed to do a great film. My

Actress Cathleen Nesbitt with my parents.

mother visited the set on several occasions, even when they were shooting on location. She enjoyed seeing Edith Head and meeting eighty-eight-year-old British actress Cathleen Nesbitt who had a small part in the picture. The film was a mild success. Afterward, Daddy would prepare for another project titled *The Short Night,* but it was very obvious that there would be no more movies for Hitch and Alma. *Family Plot* would be Hitch's last film.

~

THINGS WERE SAD for all of us as we could see both Hitch and Alma slowly fading away. Yet Mama was very present in all of our lives. "After she had a series of strokes," my daughter Katie remembers, "she still wanted to attend my high school graduation. I remember her sitting in her wheelchair, and when I looked into the audience, I saw her smiling at me with tears in her eyes. Her smile was a bit crooked from the strokes, but it didn't matter. Her love and compassion shone through that crooked smile so much that I consider that day my fondest memory of her."

We were all very good at keeping my parents company. My daughter Tere went to their home every Sunday. "I remember my grandfather being so upset about Alma–with tears in his eyes, he kept asking: 'What am I going to do?' And I would explain that he was lucky to have Grandma at home with him and when so many people had to go to the hospital. Alma was such a strong-willed person and she tried to keep on living her weekly routines, including her Thursday hair-and-nail appointment at Elizabeth Arden followed by dinner with Hitch at Chasen's."

But Daddy could not help Alma on his own; she needed the care of a nurse, and I was thrilled when we found Betty Losher, a true gem and someone who cared about my parents as if they had been her own family. She was 37 years old when she came to the house for the first time.

"On the morning of October 12, 1977, Columbus Day, the agent from the nurse's registry called and told me to go to the residence of Alfred Hitchcock," Betty remembers. "The patient was Mrs. Alfred Hitchcock. She had had a stroke some time before. I got the address and phone number and was planning on getting instructions from the night nurse. I dressed in my white uniform and arrived at the Hitchcock home around seven o'clock in the morning; I was greeted by the night nurse and by the family dog, Sarah (a West Highland White Terrier). I was led to the bedroom; on entering, the nurse went straight to the curtain and pulled it open to let some light in. I could see two figures lying in bed. One was Mr. H (he slept closest to the door); he was actually propped up, eyes closed, hands folded in front of him. Next to him was Alma (whom I called Mrs. H). Even in bed, she appeared to be very small. She propped herself up into a comfortable position and I was introduced to her–she

simply said, 'Good morning.' The night nurse showed me the medications, the bathroom, and the mirror-lined dressing room and closet. I was then introduced to Mr. H. She wished Mrs. H a good day; she replied quietly, 'Yes, thank you.' I was told that when Mrs. H. wanted breakfast, she'd ring her bell—which I had noticed on the bedside table.

I was shown around the kitchen and explained where everything was, specifically the tea and the lunch items. When I went into the walk-in refrigerator, I noticed some red Jell-O in cute little stemmed glasses. The night nurse explained how she would be back by seven in the evening and then took off. The first thing I knew about Mr. H.'s health was that he had great pain in his knees. Getting out of bed was difficult for him, but he did not complain. He explained how he had a pacemaker and had to check it periodically with a special box—and the telephone! (He later got a newer model.) His blood pressure was normal, and his pulse was always 73 beats per minute, exactly. He wore reading glasses and had problems hearing people who spoke softly. He took medication for arthritis. He was over-weight but he wasn't fat. He was generous and kind – and witty. Mrs. H, other than the results of her strokes, which had left her left side paralyzed, was in fair health. She was very alert. A physical therapist came two to three times a week and they would take a walk around the garden. Some of the routines involved doing several sets of knee bends while standing.

"I loved the Hitchcock home. It was a loving and peaceful home. Entering the front door, there was a beautiful bust of their daughter, Pat. If you turned to the right, you could see a lovely painting of Pat as a young child. To the left, there was a bar. From there, I could see that the Hitchcocks had great appreciation of fine art, literature, and gracious living. I noticed wonderful paintings by Utrillo, Klee, and Dali. There were sev-eral art books on Monet, Manet, Miro, and Bernard Buffet on display. A large piano held an amusing photograph of Mr. H with Stanley and Geoffrey, their former Sealyham Terriers. The Eight Chinese Immortals, very colorful porcelain figurines, stood vigil on the mantel of their beautiful fireplace. The sofas and chairs and other nice old pieces of furniture were placed tastefully around the room. In the far corner, an alcove with a lovely desk and chair, a built-in bookcase (I remember a few titles, *Letters to Theo Van Gogh, James Joyce's Ulysses, Florence Nightingale,* and of course several dictionaries). White carpeting was laid throughout except for one smaller rug in front of the fireplace. Through the window of one side of the living room, you could see a beautiful view of the golf green of the Bel Air Country Club. On the other side of the room was a large slid-ing glass door that opened on a patio and flower garden. The kitchen was heavenly and so well organized, one could have lived in it! There was a wine cellar, which I visited the day it was flooded.

"The relationship between Mr. and Mrs. H was a respectful, collaborative, loving, and protective one. For instance, after one of the drafts of *The Short Night* was completed, Mr. H brought a bound copy to his wife. He asked if she would read it the next day and she said she would. I remember the next morning, while Mr. H was at the 'stuuuudio,' she read the entire script, stopping only for lunch. She finished it after tea and waited for him. I was with her in the main room when he came home. He walked straight through the foyer to see his wife. 'Well, what do you think?' In her soft voice but loud enough for him to hear her, she replied, 'Quite good, quite good.' To my surprise, he completely fell apart and wept. I helped him sit next to Mrs. H. I went outside and talked to the driver. He told me that Mr. H had been worried all day about the Mrs.' opinion of the script. The next morning, I overheard Mrs. H ask, 'Whom do you see as the detective?' He immediately replied: 'Peter Lorre,' followed by, 'But we don't have him anymore.'

"They were very protective of each other. When Mr. H had a bad fall, the doctor wanted to hospitalize him to do some tests. When he went to the hospital, WE ALL WENT! Another bed was put in his room for Mrs. H. One day, a young woman therapist with her hands cupped started pounding on Mr. H's back and side. Mrs. H sat up immediately and got very upset, thinking that the woman was hurting Mr. H. We feared that Mrs. H might have another stroke so the lady left. Protective at all cost!"

~◦

MY PARENTS CONTINUED to see many of their friends: Grace Kelly, Joan Harrison, Norman Lloyd, Ernest Lehman, Hume Cronyn, and Jessica Tandy were regularly checking up on them just like I did. I'd bring them special dishes, comfy clothes, and little gifts I had made myself. I tried to be there with them as much and as often as I could.

～

IN 1978, MARY'S older daughter Melissa (Hitch and Alma's first great-granddaughter) was diagnosed with cystic fibrosis. Hitch and Alma were devastated and said that something must be done. At that time, there was little treatment and no cure. We started a foundation, and thanks to all of our efforts and the generosity of others, at the age of sixteen, Melissa underwent a living donor double lung transplant with lobes donated by her mother and her aunt Tere. We call her our miracle.

～

IN DECEMBER 1978, Hitch and Alma celebrated their fifty-second wedding anniversary and on March 7, 1979, Hitch got the Life Achievement Award from the American Film Institute. Everyone was there, and it was a very moving ceremony. My parents' nurse Betty remembers how much Alma wanted to be present.

"She was excited to go but said very little. In the morning, she told me what she wanted to wear, so I set everything out ahead of time, including her new special boots. She wore boots for support of her weak ankle. That afternoon, she put on makeup. I helped her with her hair. She sometimes wore a fashionable wig. When I pulled out the boots, she decided she wanted to wear heels. I didn't want to contradict her, but I was afraid she would injure herself. We tried to make a few steps with the high-heels shoes, but it was too painful. So luckily, she agreed to put on the new pair of boots. That night, I watched the show on television. I was so proud. And I knew how proud she was for Mr. H."

～

WHEN DADDY MADE his speech, all he could think of was Mama:

"I beg permission to mention by name only four people who have given me the most affection, appreciation, encouragement, and constant collaboration. The first of the four is a film editor, the second is a script writer, the third is the mother of my daughter, Pat, and the fourth is as fine a cook as ever performed miracles in a domestic kitchen, and their names are Alma Reville. Had the beautiful Miss Reville not accepted a lifetime contract, without options, as Mrs. Alfred Hitchcock some fifty-three years ago, Mr. Alfred Hitchcock might not be in this room tonight—not at this table but as one of the slow waiters on the floor. I share this award, as I have my life, with her."

⁓

ON MAY 8, Hitch decided it was time to close the office at Universal. To ease his pain, he sent his good friend and colleague Hilton Green to tell Mr. Wasserman. On December 31, Daddy was made knight of the British Empire, and on January 3, 1980, he officially became Sir Alfred Hitchcock. Mama and I were so proud. But Hitch's health was declining rapidly—he was refusing to eat. We had a male nurse with him at all times, and he was moved to the guest bedroom. Finally, on April 29, 1980, Daddy died peacefully in his sleep at 8:35 in the morning. I was the one who told Mama. I left her alone with him for a little while. I remember she said nothing; she held his left hand in her right hand. She leaned over and kissed it. Then, we took her back to the bedroom. Daddy's funeral took place at the Church of the Good Shepherd in Beverly Hills. It was a very sad day. As he had requested, Hitch was cremated at the Live Oak Crematory in Monrovia, California. His ashes were spread off the California coast in the Pacific Ocean. On May 3, Oliver Kelly said a mass in Hitch's memory at Westminster Cathedral. Alma would survive Daddy for two more years.

"The morning of my grandfather's death, I remember walking into her room," my daughter Mary remembers. "She was sitting in her wheelchair and staring out the window. It was very

My daughters Tere and Katie with Alma, Hitch and myself after my parents' 75th birthday dinner.

sad to see her looking so old and frail and now without him. From that day, she retreated mentally back to a better life. It was easier for her to think he was still alive than to accept that he was gone. We all went along with her stories and tried to make her life as comfortable as possible. Her days were spent watching television, reading, and being visited by all of us."

Alma died on July 6, 1982, the day before my birthday. Her funeral was held at St. Paul the Apostle Church in Westwood, California. Like Hitch, Alma was cremated, and her ashes were thrown at sea. During this difficult time, one article appeared that filled me with pride and happiness. It was published on July 29, 1982, and written by film critic Charles Champlin in the *Los Angeles Times*. The article was titled, "Alma Reville Hitchcock—The Unsung Partner." I was very grateful and pleased about the article. Mr. Champlin felt that Alma's death had been "underreported" and was compelled to write a long article about her

career and her life at Daddy's side. He was the one who came up with a quote that I think summarizes best the Alfred/Alma Hitchcock legacy. He wrote: "The Hitchcock touch had four hands, and two were Alma's."

The name Hitchcock will never be forgotten. But for my daughters and myself, in addition to the wonderful legacy of the movies left behind, we have the personal memories as well. They're not necessarily what one might think of as the typical glamorous Hollywood memories. They're very simple and yet, as my daughter Tere says, they'll always be with us. "My favorite memories of Alma are the times we spent together alone. She was so fair that she always made a point of spending alone time with my sisters and I separate. I loved driving with her, stopping along

the road for a picnic. I simply loved watching her take care of the garden, cooking, reading, and relaxing. There was such peace about her. I also remember her taking me to Elizabeth Arden. I was always on my best behavior, although one day, I completely shocked her; we were at a department store and I told her that my ambition was to become an elevator operator. As I grew older, both Hitch and Alma were always curious about what I did. I got a job at McDonald's, and they were fascinated by the notion of fast food. They wanted to know everything about it. They were truly genuinely nice; they loved people and animals. When my pet rabbit Fred died, they were the first ones to call; they understood my pain and immediately invited me to come spend the night with them. I still miss them after all these years. To this day, along with my mother and my two sisters, I still admire Alma's character. She had such self-esteem and confidence that she never needed to draw any attention to herself. I have raised my children to be who they are and accept themselves without thinking about what others might think. This, to me, epitomizes who Alma truly was."

~o

ALMA AND HITCH are still with us. I make every effort to personally appear at any events honoring my parents' work, even when it sometimes means dealing with people who want to engage you on the dark side of the track.

My dear husband Joe died of a heart attack on January 21, 1994. I miss him every day, and I thank God for my three beautiful daughters, their amazing husbands, and their loving children.

When Alma died, she looked peacefully asleep. That's one of the images I keep of her. I knew then she was happy. She was back with Daddy—reunited at last, laughing at a few jokes, enjoying good food, talking about the good old days, but most of all, watching over us as they always did.

Daddy, Mama, I love you. Your daughter, Pat.

To Catch a Meal: Alma's Cookbook

ℱOOD WAS AS important in my father's films as it was on the table at home and overall in my parents' life. Although, critics and film historians were quick to read a lot more than there was, in the fact that food in a Hitchcock film was often substitute for sex or was inevitably linked to marriage and murder. My father once said, "There will obviously be a lot of drama in the steak that is too rare." Truthfully speaking, in making films that often dealt with violence, sex, and murder, filmmakers of the past had to find a clever way to convey such graphic themes without showing anything offensive. One thing that my father certainly knew well was food and, therefore, he used it at length to substitute for images that the censors of the

Two of my parents' favorite dinner guests—Peggy and Norman Lloyd.

time would not allow him to show. Also, let's not forget that his father had owned a grocery store. People often ask: Did Alma like food as much as my father? She loved to cook more than she liked to eat. The one image that sticks in my mind is seeing how slow she was at the table. My father and I would just gobble up our food. Alma didn't eat a lot; and still, we were always done before she was.

As I already mentioned several times, my parents loved to entertain their friends. Lew Wasserman remembered: "I have many fond memories of Alma. She was a wonderful woman, great friend, and spectacular cook. Dinner with Alma and Hitch at their home was an invitation Edie and I looked forward to and eagerly accepted. I remember one particular night when the dinner Alma made seemed especially delicious. I complimented her on it, and she said if I came into the kitchen with her, she'd let me have more. I didn't need any prodding and gladly followed her into the other room. I expected her to open the oven and give me a second portion. Instead, she swung open the refrigerator and handed me a frozen dinner!!" Although rarely the instigator, Mama liked to joke around with her friends.

~

MY PARENTS WERE also great wine connoisseurs and collectors. Few people know that Daddy was a Grand Officer of the Burgundian Order of Tastevin, meaning he was tapped on the shoulder by an aged wine root and could meet up to four times a year in the cloister of Clos Vougeot in Burgundy, France to consume as much fine Burgundy wine as he could carry. At one point, my parents had 1,600 bottles of imported wine, including some 1890 vintage. My parents took wine very seriously; their favorite red was Romanee Conti; their favorite white was Montrachet. "You don't suppose I waste good wine on my guests," Hitch once declared jokingly. "Good wine is to be drunk on one's own. Conversation is the enemy of good wine and food. It is quite pointless to serve either at a dinner party. . . ." At the same time, my parents loved to send wine as gifts to their friends and colleagues. Mel Brooks had done a parody of my father's films titled *High Anxiety* (1978). It was hilarious, and my parents loved both the film and Mel. They had lunch at Chasen's and became good friends—which entitled Mel to receive a pricey case of wine.

By the mid-sixties, Daddy's off-screen schedule was, in Mama's own words, "conducted like a railroad timetable." When he was in the middle of a movie, he would be in bed by 10 o'clock. He'd wake up around 3 in the morning and spend an hour thinking about the next day's work. He then went back to sleep and woke up at 7. Alma pretty much followed the same routine—except for the part that took place at 3 in the morning. Hitch and Alma would have a very simple breakfast, usually just coffee. After his lunch on the set, Hitch had made a habit of calling Alma to discuss dinner. By the end of the conversation, everything was set and he knew what he would find on the table when he got home.

Daddy and the Lloyds enjoying an early dinner outside. Our housekeeper Chrystal was helping Mama out and serving bread rolls.

If you'd ask Hitch what his favorite room in the house was, he would have said the kitchen. One reason was because Mama was often in there, another was her cooking. Alma loved to cook; but above all, she loved to cook for Hitch. His favorite dinner was roast chicken and boiled ham. One day, a friend was visiting and noticed how much food Alma was preparing. The friend asked, "How many people are you expecting tonight?" Alma replied nonchalantly, "That's just for the two of us." Dinners took all evening, especially when work at the studio was slow. My mother once told me about one day when she had found a roast-duck recipe she wanted to try. She discussed it with Hitch over breakfast. She knew better than to surprise him; she couldn't take the chance of him not liking it. Also, it couldn't wait until the 3 o'clock call; Mama had to get to work.

When Daddy came home that evening, Alma was setting the kitchen table with a handmade linen cloth, their best silver, and thin-stem glasses. Daddy strung the beans and then he discussed with Alma which wine would go best with duck; they had their soup and then the main course. They took their time, and at the end of the dinner, after a cup of coffee, Hitch stood up, put on an apron, filled the sink with water, sprinkled the soap, and did the dishes. Alma offered to help, but he wouldn't hear of it. Before they left the kitchen that night, they looked at each other and said, "Best evening ever!" Alma loved to go to restaurants, copy recipes, and try them at home. She and I shared the same passion; I'd give her my own recipes, and she'd give me hers. She also wrote elaborate menus for when they entertained guests.

However, there was one dish my mother would not serve to my father: eggs. He absolutely hated eggs: "I loathe the living sight of them," he once said. His hatred for eggs was obvious at home, but also in his films: In *To Catch a Thief,* he had a single shot of the character played by Jesse Royce Landis crushing a cigarette, not in an ashtray, but in eggs served sunny side up! In *Spellbound,* Constance, the psychiatrist portrayed by Ingrid Bergman, says: "I'm glad you didn't dream about me as an egg beater, as one of my patients did." In *Sabotage,* the little boy named Stevie (Desmond Tester) says, "He is too dignified to eat eggs." And later, the character played by John Loder says, "Poached eggs, here at Simpson's? Well, it's enough to make the roast beef turn until it's gravy!"

Alma agreed with Hitch that cinema was their life, but food played a big role in it as well. Food was the opportunity for them to be together and to enjoy the simplicity of life. After all, it was Hitch who said, "Cinema is not a slice of life, it's a piece of cake." And what made it a "piece of cake" was Alma.

There was always room at our table for guests—even canine ones.

My parents always loved eating a good meal outside during a beautiful day with friends and family.

⁓

$\mathcal{T}$HE FOLLOWING ARE some of my mother's most treasured recipes. As I've mentioned before, Mama was a wonderful cook and enjoyed experimenting with different ingredients and techniques. She learned many of them by watching various chefs cook, and she was really skillful at changing them to suit our family's tastes. Mama was also very good at changing measurements and quantities as she went along, or kind of estimating amounts according to what she felt like. She often did not even specify quantities in many of her recipes. While some of the ingredients may be harder to find nowadays, I present these recipes in their original form in order to stay true to what my parents, Alma and Hitch, enjoyed in our home as I was growing up.

VICHYSSOISE SOUP

2 onions
3 leeks
6 potatoes, sliced
1 gallon broth
2 tablespoons flour
Butter
Cream
Salt
Chives
Nutmeg

SLIGHTLY BROWN the onions and the leeks in butter. Put these and the sliced potatoes into the broth. Thicken with the flour. Cook for 40 minutes until the potatoes have fallen apart. Strain, and cool. Add some heavy cream and salt to taste. Before serving sprinkle with chopped chives and a little nutmeg.

DOUBLE CONSOMME

MAKES 4 QUARTS

4 pounds lean beef, chopped
6 ounces carrots, diced fine
6 ounces leeks, diced fine
2 egg whites
5 quarts white consomme (page 235)

$\mathscr{P}$UT CHOPPED meat and diced carrots and leeks into a deep pot and add egg whites. Mix together. Pour the cold consomme into the pot and bring to a boil, stirring frequently. Lower heat when boiling to the simmering stage and let simmer for 1½ hours. Strain through a napkin and fill 8 small 1 pint plastic cartons. Freeze.

WHITE CONSOMME

Makes 5½ Quarts

4 pounds lean beef (rump roast)
3 pounds beef knuckle (with bone)
2 tablespoons salt
4 large carrots
3 turnips
1 parsnip
4 leeks (tied in a bundle)
1 sprig of thyme
1 medium onion
¼ bay leaf

TIE THE meat with a string, put in a big earthenware stock pot, and add 8 quarts of water. Bring to a boil. When boiling, skim muck off the top. Add 2 tablespoons salt. Put in all the vegetables and herbs and simmer just below boiling for 5 hours. Cool. Remove fat and fine strain into cartons.

VEAL AND HAM PIE (COLD)

¾ cup leaf lard
3 cups flour
½ teaspoon salt
Cooked veal and ham (save liquid from veal)
Salt and pepper
Butter

𝒫LACE LEAF lard in a saucepan with a pinch of salt. Bring to a quick boil for 3 or 4 minutes over a brisk flame. Stir in all at once, flour sifted with ½ teaspoon salt, stirring constantly until the mixture leaves the sides of the pan. Remove from fire and continue to stir until the dough is cool enough to knead. Place the cooked dough on a floured board and knead until it is perfectly smooth. Cover with a dry cloth and let it stand in a warm place for 30 minutes. Then knead again for 2 minutes.

Roll out two thirds of the dough and line a springform mold with it. Fill it with previously cooked veal and ham, cut into small pieces. Season with salt and pepper. Strain some of the liquid the veal has been cooked in and pour over the filling to within about 1 inch of the top. Dot the surface of the meat with small pieces of butter. Roll out the remaining dough large enough to cover the springform and overlap the sides. Moisten the edges and crimp them together securely with your fingers. Make a hole in the center of the top crust and bake in a slow oven (300°) for 2 hours, brushing the top with beaten egg mixed with a little milk, 30 minutes before removing from oven. Place in refrigerator for at least 6 hours before serving.

STEAK AND KIDNEY PUDDING

12 ounces flour
1 pound suet
1 teaspoon baking powder
¼ teaspoon salt
½ pint water
2 pounds steak
1 pound beef kidney
Salt and pepper

SUET PASTE

Mix flour, suet (grated), baking powder, ¼ teaspoon salt with ½ pint water until it is a moderately stiff paste. Line a pudding basin with it, keeping some back for a cover.

CUT THE steak and beef kidney into 2-inch pieces, sprinkle with flour, salt, and pepper, and put them in layers in the lined basin. Fill about three quarters full with boiling water. Cover with the rest of the suet paste. Tie over a floured cloth. Lower gently into a saucepan of boiling water, being careful that no water is allowed to come over the basin. Keep boiling gently for 5 to 7 hours. It may need more water added from time to time. Remove from pan, take off cloth, and fasten a serviette around the basin to serve.

CHICKEN PÂTÉ

½ pound chicken livers
Butter
¼ cup chopped onions
Salt and pepper
¼ teaspoon thyme
¼ teaspoon marjoram, basil, and sage
¼ cup brandy

CUT CHICKEN livers in quarters; brown in butter; add chopped onions, and cook for 2 minutes. Add salt, pepper, thyme, ¼ teaspoon marjoram, basil, sage, mixed, and brandy. Blend until smooth and pack.

STUFFING PATTIES FOR CHICKEN

2 cups grated beef suet
1 cup bread crumbs
1 teaspoon mixed herbs
Flour
1 egg, beaten
Chopped parsley
Salt and pepper

Mɪx ᴛʜᴇ suet and bread crumbs, a good teaspoon of mixed herbs, salt, and pepper. Bind together with a beaten egg, with a *lot* of chopped parsley. Make into smallish rissoles, roll in flour lightly, and sauté in butter on high flame until brown, then simmer until needed.

POULET À LA VALLEE D'AUGE

2 (3-pound) broilers (chickens)
Salt and pepper
¼ pound butter
4 tablespoons Calvados or applejack brandy
5 or 6 shallots
1 tablespoon chopped parsley
1 sprig thyme or ¼ teaspoonful dried thyme
½ cup white wine
½ cup heavy cream

CUT TWO broilers as for frying, and salt and pepper them. Brown them lightly on all sides in butter. Lower the flame and continue to cook for 15 minutes, turning the pieces often. Pour in warmed Calvados or applejack brandy, light it, and shake the pan until the flame dies down. Add shallots, finely chopped, chopped parsley, thyme, and white wine. Blend well, cover, and cook until chicken is tender. Arrange the chicken on a heated platter. Add heavy cream to the liquid in the pan, heat, and pour this aromatic sauce over the chicken before serving.

STEWED STEAK

1 large sliced onion
4 tablespoons butter
2 pounds top sirloin
2 large tomatoes
3 tablespoons flour
Bunch of young carrots
Chopped celery
Salt
Pepper
Lump of sugar
½ pound mushrooms
3 tablespoons red wine

FRY ONE large sliced onion in butter. Cut top sirloin steak into about 2-inch pieces. When onions are golden brown, put them in a casserole dish. Fry the steak in the same pan with more butter, over very hot flame, until brown on all sides, then add these to casserole. Meanwhile, have two large tomatoes cooking in water. Add 2 more tablespoons of butter into frying pan with flour and mix well. Add the strained tomatoes and some stock (or water if stock is not available) and stir well over a flame. Add salt, pepper, and a lump of sugar. Cut up a bunch of young carrots and add to the casserole. Strain the thick gravy from the frying pan into the casserole and cook in a slow oven (250–300°) for 3 to 4 hours. About 1 hour before serving, add mushrooms and a little chopped celery. Ten minutes before serving, add 3 tablespoons red wine.

FILET DE BOEUF EN GELEE
(ROAST TENDERLOIN IN ASPIC)

SERVES 8

1 pound short ribs
1 pound bottom round roast
4 pounds shank bones
3 carrots, peeled
3 turnips, peeled
⅓ cup port
2 egg whites and their shells
4 pounds tenderloin of beef
3 tablespoons butter, softened
Salt, to taste

𝒯HE DAY before serving, fill a large saucepan with cold, salted water. Add the short ribs, bottom round roast, shank bones, and veal bones. Skim all fat off assiduously while bringing the pan to the boil. Add the peeled vegetables and cook for 4 hours, covered, over medium heat. Reserve the bones, meats and vegetables. Add the port and boil down to concentrate the flavor of the broth. There should be about 2 quarts of it. Refrigerate this bouillon overnight. Scrape off the fat accumulated on the surface. To clarify this bouillon, beat 1 cup cold bouillon into the egg whites and their shells. Bring the rest of the bouillon to a boil. Add some of the hot broth to the cold mixture, then pour it all back into the pan. Bring it to a simmer, stirring constantly, then maintain at a quiet simmer without stirring for 15 minutes.

(Preheat oven to 425°). Line a large strainer with several layers of clean cheesecloth and strain the broth through it. Spread the tenderloin with butter and roast for about 30 minutes for rare meat. Let the meat cool and carve into slices. Arrange in a not-too-deep serving dish so they overlap. Pour the broth over the slices and refrigerate to jell overnight.

PREPARATION TIME: 30 MINUTES
COOKING TIME: 5½ HOURS
JELLING TIME: ABOUT 12 HOURS

BEEF BEAUJOLAIS

2 tablespoons bacon fat
2 pounds lean beef, bottom or, preferable,
top round cut in 2-inch squares
2 medium onions, minced
6 shallots, minced
1 tablespoon flour
Salt and pepper, to taste
2 carrots, quartered
2 large bay leaves
1 heaping teaspoon thyme
1½ cups Beaujolais
½ cup Madeira
½ pound mushrooms, stems and caps
2 tablespoons butter
1 liqueur glass brandy
6 carrots, cut small
12 white pearl onions
4 tablespoons parsley, minced
6 new potatoes

COOKING TIME: 3 TO 4 HOURS APPROXIMATELY

HEAT BACON fat in heavy pan, add beef, and brown over light heat. Remove meat to heavy casserole. Sauté onions and shallots in original pan until tender; sprinkle with flour and salt, and cook for 3 minutes. Add carrots, herbs, pepper, red wine, Madeira, and sliced mushroom stems to meat. Cover and simmer gently 3 to 4 hours or until tender (add a little wine occasionally if necessary to keep meat almost covered with liquid). Remove meat to another casserole, then pass sauce through sieve and pour over meat. Sauté sliced mushroom caps in butter for 5 minutes and add to stew. Heat brandy, set aflame, and when flame goes out, add to stew. Then add 6 carrots, onions, sprinkle with parsley, and serve with new boiled potatoes or riced potatoes.

SUGGESTED WINE: Choose a good Beaujolais such as Moulin a Vent, and use the same wine for cooking and drinking.

BOEUF EN CROUTE (BEEF WELLINGTON)

SERVES FOUR

2 pounds fillet of beef (in one piece)
1 large (½ lb.) packet puff pastry (frozen)
2 ounces butter, to taste
1 small can liver pâté
½ lb. mushrooms, chopped
Salt and pepper, to taste
2 tablespoons milk

𝒫REHEAT OVEN to 425°. Trim fat and skin from fillet. Roll out pastry very thinly to give piece 1¼ times the length of the fillet and wide enough to wrap around it with a good overlap. Spread the fillet all over with slightly softened butter. Lightly spread some pâté where the meat is to lie along the middle of the pastry, and cover with chopped mushrooms, and season lightly. Place fillet on top of mushrooms. Bring up the sides of the pastry to make a neat roll, and seal the edges together by moistening with a little milk, making a ridge on the top, which can be decoratively slashed. Seal the ends tightly. Place on a baking pan on middle shelf of oven for 20 minutes at 425°. If browning too quickly, cover with foil. After 20 minutes, remove the boeuf en croute and turn the oven down to 350°. Brush the top with a little milk to glaze it. Cover lightly with foil and put back in oven for 25 minutes (the heat of the oven will be reducing for a while so should be left at 350°. After 45 minutes of total cooking time, you should have a really rare beef within the crust. If you prefer it a little more well done, leave it in another 10 minutes.

Serve it as soon as possible when done as the beef goes on cooking in the crust if you keep it warm, cut slices about an inch crosswise.

POMMES DE TERRE SOUFFLES

$\mathcal{P}$EEL SOME Dutch or Spanish (floury) potatoes and wipe them
dry. Then, cut them into round slices ¾ inch thick, which also
must be dried in a cloth. Heat fat in two deep-frying saucepans.
One must be hot but not boiling, and the potato slices should
be plunged into it and remain 7 or 8 minutes. Then drain the fat
quickly from the potato slices and plunge them into the second
saucepan, which must be boiling. The potato slices swell; when
they are golden-brown and firm, let them drain and sprinkle
with salt.

MOUSSE DE SOLE AU CHAMPAGNE

2 pounds English soles—about four soles (boned)
3 teaspoons salt
A little pepper
4 egg whites
1 quart heavy cream

POUND THE fish with salt and pepper, gradually adding the egg whites. Strain through a fine sieve and into a saucepan on ice. Then, work it up with a wooden spoon and gradually fold in the cream. Mold the mousse into a buttered mold and place mold in a pan of hot water. Cook it in the oven over hot water at 350° for 1 hour.

SAUCE CHAMPAGNE

TAKE THE BONES from the soles used for the mousse and place in a buttered pan with ½ chopped onion, 2 chopped shallots, and salt and pepper to taste. Cover with white dry wine or champagne and boil slowly. Cook down mixture until reduced, thicken with 2 or 3 spoons of Veloute of fish, or if unable, 2 or 3 spoons bechamel (white cream sauce). Add 1 pint heavy cream, finally adding 2 tablespoons of melted butter and juice from 2 lemons. Strain the sauce and pour over the mousse. Use sliced truffles for decorating.

Sauce Americaine for Mousse de Sole
1 cooked lobster (2 pounds)
1 tablespoon salt, chopped
Pepper
½ cup olive oil
4 tablespoons butter
1 shallot, chopped
1 small white onion, chopped
1 clove garlic, crushed
1 small glass cognac
1 glass dry white wine
1 cup fish stock
2 fresh tomatoes
2 tablespoons tomato purée
10 leaves fresh tarragon
Cayenne pepper
Parsley, chopped

CUT THE LOBSTER in pieces (put aside the creamy part and coral). Season the lobster with salt and pepper, sauté pieces with olive oil and butter in a deep saucepan. Remove the fat, add shallot, onion, and crushed garlic. Flambe with cognac, add white wine, fish stock, tomatoes, tomato purée, tarragon, cayenne, and parsley. Cover tightly and let boil for 20 to 25 minutes. Remove the lobster to another dish. Reduce the cooking sauce to half. Add the creamy parts and coral together with butter. Let cook for a moment. Pass through a strainer and season to taste. Serve this sauce on the side.

FISH MOUSSE WITH PIKE

MAKES 8 SERVINGS

¾ *pound filet of sole*
2 pounds filet of pike (or other white fish)
2½ teaspoons salt
¼ teaspoon nutmeg
⅛ teaspoon thyme
¼ teaspoon liquid pepper seasoning
½ teaspoon powdered savory
6 unbeaten egg whites
3 cups very well chilled heavy cream
(If you wish, use ⅔ cup dry white wine and
decrease the cream to 2½ cups.)

𝒫UT THE raw fish fillets through the finest blade of a meat grinder three times. Add the seasonings and egg whites (and wine if you use it). Mix well and then put the fish through the food mill or coarse strainer two more times. Discard the parts that will not go through each time. Chill the mixture for 1 hour, then gradually blend in the cream. Turn the mixture into a buttered six-cup mold or loaf pan. Place in a pan of hot water in a moderate oven, 350°F, then bake for 1 hour and 15 minutes. Remove from the oven and allow to stand for 5 minutes before unfolding. Drain of liquid that forms from the mold and add to the sauce. Serve immediately.

YORKSHIRE PUDDING
(Mr. Hitchcock's Special Own)

2 eggs
1 cup milk
½ teaspoon salt
1 cup flour
1 tablespoon Crisco vegetable shortening

$\mathcal{P}$UT TWO eggs in a blender alone. Keep the blender going while you add the milk and the salt. Add the flour teaspoon by teaspoon. Give it a final good whirl at top speed. Put blender and contents in refrigerator until ready to cook.

Put large tablespoon of Crisco in a small baking pan and place in 400° oven. When it is *very* hot, take blender from the refrigerator, give it another good whirl at high speed for a moment, then pour it into the hot pan with the Crisco. Put back into the oven.

Pudding should take about 15 minutes to rise. Leave it in the oven until it dries out. Once it has risen, you might be able to turn heat down to 350°—but care should be taken about this.

ALMOND SOUFFLÉ

3 tablespoons butter
2 tablespoons flour
1 cup milk
¼ teaspoon salt
½ cup sugar
Almond extract
4 egg yolks, lightly beaten
5 egg whites, stiffly beaten

MELT BUTTER in a saucepan and blend well with flour. Gradually add milk, stirring constantly, and mix in salt, sugar, and almond extract. When the sauce is thick and smooth, remove from fire and cool. Add lightly beaten egg yolks and beat well. Fold in stiffly beaten egg whites.

Butter a soufflé dish, sprinkle it with sugar, and pour in the batter. Set the dish in a pan of hot, boiling water. Bake in a hot oven (400°) for 15 minutes, reduce the heat to moderate (375°), and cook for 20 to 25 minutes longer.

FROZEN VANILLA SOUFFLE

Serves 8 to 10

4 egg yolks
1 cup sugar
⅛ teaspoon salt
1 cup milk
4 inch piece vanilla bean or 1½ teaspoons pure vanilla
1 cup light cream
2 cups heavy cream, whipped

ℬᴇᴀᴛ ᴇɢɢ yolks in the top of a double boiler until light and lemon-colored. Gradually beat in sugar. Stir in salt and ¼ cup milk.

Split the vanilla bean. Place it in a saucepan with the light cream and remaining milk. Heat until scalded. Cool.

Remove the vanilla bean. Gradually stir the milk mixture into the egg mixture. Cook over hot (not boiling) water, stirring constantly, until the mixture coats a metal spoon. Cool.

Fold in whipped cream. Turn into a 1-quart soufflé dish with a 3-inch band of heavy brown paper or foil tied around the outside at the top. This will give the mixture the illusion of a hot soufflé when frozen.

Place in a freezer for 6 to 8 hours or overnight. Remove the paper rim and serve from the dish. Garnish with shaved chocolate or powdered cocoa.

SOUFFLE L'UN ET L'AUTRE

$\mathcal{I}$N TWO DIFFERENT bowls, make two soufflé mixtures—one chocolate and one coffee. Put it into a soufflé dish, separating the two flavors with a piece of strong paper (oiled) across the width.

Put it in a hot oven (425°) for 25 minutes. At the end of 10 minutes cooking time, remove the paper.

CREPES ELIZABETH

1⅛ cups of flour
4 tablespoons sugar
Salt
3 eggs
1½ cups of milk
Butter
1 tablespoon Kirsch
2 tablespoons strawberries
Almonds

SIFT FLOUR, sugar, and a pinch of salt into a mixing bowl. Beat eggs lightly, stir them into milk, and gradually stir the combined liquid into the dry ingredients. Continue to stir until batter is smooth. It should just coat a spoon. If it is too thick, stir in a little more milk. Stir in 1 tablespoon each of melted butter and Kirsch, and let stand for 1 to 2 hours.

Heat a small frying pan, 5 to 6 inches in diameter. Put in ½ teaspoon butter and swirl the pan to coat the bottom and the sides. Pour in about 2 tablespoonsful of the above batter and again tilt the pan in a circular motion to spread the batter evenly and thinly to the edges. Cook for about 1 minute or until set and brown on the underside, turn, and brown the other side. Crepes must be cooked quickly to be at their best. Slide each finished crepes onto a warm platter and continue to make until all the batter is used.

Place 2 tablespoons sliced and sugared strawberries in the center of each crepe and roll it to enclose the filling. Put the rolled crepes in a shallow, buttered, ovenproof dish, sprinkle with blanched almonds, shredded and buttered, and put them under a broiler flame until the crepes blister. Serve hot with whipped cream sweetened and flavored to taste.

DINING AT THE HITCHCOCKS':
ALMA'S MENUS FOR 1963

Dinner for Tippi Hedren
(Return of our European promotion trip for 'The Birds'   Sept. 20th 1963
Extra help: Chrystal.

Cocktails.

Caviare - Toast.
Foie Gras.
Rainbow Trout.

—

Vichyssoise Soup.
(Rolls.)

Trout en gelee.
(Watercress Rolls.)
Roast Pheasant.
Braised Celery.
Bread Sauce

Gravy.

—

Aspine Gatto.

—

Coffee
Liquors.

January 18, 1963

~⌐

Dinner party for five, for Tippi Hedren's birthday.
Extra help: Chrystal, Rose
Cocktails
Mushroom appetizer
Cheese rolls
Wine and champagne

~⌐

MENU:

♦ Pâté Maison
♦ Turtle Soup
♦ Cheese Straws
♦ Fillets of Sole Meuniere
♦ Watercress Rolls
♦ Wine: Corton Charlemagne
♦ Stripper of Beef
♦ Small Roast Potatoes
♦ String Beans
♦ Gravy

WINE: GRAND ECHELAN

♦ Strawberries in Pineapple
♦ English Cream
♦ Birthday Duke of Windsor
♦ Peach Cup
♦ Coffee and Liquors

January 23, 1963

∽

Dinner for eight for Universal executives, sales department
(after showing of The Birds*).*
Extra help: Chrystal, Rose
Cocktails: One bottle of Pouilly Frussie, Scotch, Bourbon, Vodka
Wine: One bottle of Le Montrachet (1957),
three bottles of La Tache (1957)
Canapes

∽

MENU:

- ◆ Pâté Maison or Smoked Salmon
- ◆ Boeuf Beaujolais
- ◆ Small white potatoes, peas, brussel sprouts
- ◆ Cheese, French bread, crackers
- ◆ Pickwick ice pudding
- ◆ Coffee, liquors

January 27, 1963

~

Dinner for Ed Henry and his wife.
(Ed Henry was an agent.)
No help.

~

MENU:

+ Cocktails, party snacks
+ Steak and kidney pudding
+ String beans
+ Mashed potatoes
+ Pears Hêlene
+ Ice cream, chocolate sauce
+ Coffee, liquors

January 30, 1963

～

Dinner for three for Samuel Taylor (screenwriter, Vertigo, Topaz*).*
Extra help: Chrystal
Cocktails

～

MENU:

♦ Spinach soup, French Bread
♦ Stripper on spit
♦ Brown potato balls
♦ String beans
♦ Gravy
♦ Cheese
♦ Pineapple
♦ Coffee

February 3, 1963

~⌒

Dinner for three for Samuel Taylor.
No help.
Cocktails, martinis

~⌒

MENU:

- ◆ Pâté fois gras, toast
  - ◆ French ox tail
- ◆ Peas, carrots, potatoes
  - ◆ Pears Hêlene
    - ◆ Coffee

February 9, 1963

~

Dinner for six for Don Frost (Bristol Myers Sponsor, TV).
Extra help: Chrystal, Rose

~

MENU:

♦ Caviar, toast
♦ Vodka
♦ Fillet Dover sole
♦ Watercress rolls
♦ Wine: Haut Brion Blanc (1958)
♦ Saddle baby lamb
♦ Peas, small white potatoes, gravy

WINE: CH. BEYCHEVELLE (1945)

♦ Raspberry sherbet crepes

CHAMPAGNE: DOM PERIGNON (1952)

♦ Cheese
♦ Coffee, liquors: brandy, Cordon Argent

February 10, 1963

~

Brunch for three for Samuel Taylor.

~

MENU:

+ Grapefruit
+ Quiche Lorraine
+ Salad
+ French bread

February 14th · 1963 .   Dinner for Wassermans
(4)

Menu.

Spinach Soup.

Scallopini of Veal.   Montrachet
Sauté Potatoes .   ('57)
String Beans.

Fresh Strawberries .
English Cream.

Coffee .

February 16, 1963

~⌒

Dinner for three for Samuel Taylor

~⌒

MENU:

- Turtle soup
- Wine: Chateau Chalon
- Lamb chops
- Potatoes, asparagus

WINE: MOUTON ROTHSCHILD

- Strawberries, cream
- Coffee

February 27, 1963

~❀

Dinner for four for Mr. and Mrs. Pollock.
Extra help: Chrystal, Rose

~❀

MENU:

- ◆ Pâté
- ◆ Mushroom soup
- ◆ Stripper
- ◆ Peas in artichoke bases
- ◆ Gravy
- ◆ Duke of Windsor
- ◆ Coffee, liquors

April 3, 1963

~⌒

Lunch for three for Bill Fry and Jerry Adler (TV).
Extra help: Chrystal

~⌒

MENU:

* ♦ Melon
* ♦ Escallop of veal
* ♦ Sautéed potatoes
* ♦ String beans

WINE: CHATEAU DE SELLE

* ♦ Strawberries and cream
* ♦ Coffee

Weekend in Santa Cruz, April 12, 13, & 14, 1963

Joan Harrison and husband, Eric Ambler, and Samuel Taylor.
Extra help: Chrystal

FRIDAY, DINNER:

+ Spinach soup
+ Santa Cruz fish
+ Allumette potatoes
+ Artichokes
+ Pears Hêlene

SATURDAY, LUNCH:

+ Melon
+ Irish ham with Madeira sauce
+ Purée of peas
+ Pommes purée
+ Strawberries, crème double

SATURDAY, DINNER:

+ Pâté maison (with cocktails)
+ Roast ducks
+ Apple sauce, peas, new potatoes
+ "Pickwick" ice pudding
+ Coffee

SUNDAY BRUNCH:

+ Grapefruit
+ Mixed grill (bacon, sausages, kidneys, tomatoes, mushrooms, popovers)
+ Pineapple

SUNDAY DINNER:

+ English turbot, hollandaise sauce
+ Saddle of lamb
+ Asparagus, roast potatoes
+ Vanilla ring with peaches, raspberry sauce
+ Coffee, liquors

Weekend at Santa Cruz, July 4, 5, 6, & 7, 1963

~~

Jay Presson Allen and husband Lewis Allen.
Extra help: Chrystal and extra help

~~

THURSDAY BREAKFAST:

♦ Coffee, tea, coffee cakes, juice

THURSDAY LUNCH:

♦ Melon
♦ Irish ham, Madeira sauce
♦ Purée of peas, pommes purée
♦ Stew strawberries, Jersey cream

THURSDAY DINNER:

♦ Mushroom soup
♦ Saddle of lamb, mint sauce
♦ String beans, squash, roast potatoes
♦ Deep dish apple blackberry pie, whipped cream

FRIDAY LUNCH:

♦ Cold lobsters, mayonnaise
♦ Pâté en croute, salad
♦ Caramel custard cream

FRIDAY DINNER:

- ◆ Spinach soup
- ◆ Santa Cruz fish
- ◆ Fried potatoes (thin), artichokes
- ◆ English trifle

SATURDAY LUNCH:

- ◆ Jellied consommé
- ◆ Cold roast beef, salad
- ◆ Fresh raspberries in pineapple

SATURDAY DINNER:

- ◆ Celery soup
- ◆ Roast ducks
- ◆ Apple sauce, new potatoes, peas
- ◆ Alpine grotto

SUNDAY LUNCH:

- ◆ Grapefruit, rolls, etc.
- ◆ Porterhouse steaks on barbecue
- ◆ Potatoes in jackets
- ◆ Asparagus
- ◆ Cold fruit mousse

Monday. July 8th. 1963. Crystal sedia beep.
Dinner for 4. Sir Christopher Chancellor - (T.V.)

MENU.

Pate Maison.

Sauteed Trout
Watercress Rolls.

Roast Chickens with
Cream Sauce.
mushrooms in patty cases.
Petit Pois
New Potatoes

Duke of Windsor

Coffee - Liqueurs

July 31, 1963

~

Dinner for seven for Mrs. Joseph O'Connell.
Extra help: Chrystal

~

MENU:

- ◆ Caviar canapes
- ◆ Celery soup, rolls
- ◆ Salmon trout, Hollandaise sauce
- ◆ New Maine potatoes
- ◆ Saddle of lamb, mint sauce
- ◆ Roast potatoes, peas in zucchini
- ◆ Fruit salad
- ◆ Duke of Windsor
- ◆ Coffee

$\mathcal{S}$*eptember 20, 1963*

~~

Dinner for Tippi Hedren, return from European
Promotion Trip for The Birds.
Extra help: Chrystal

~~

MENU:

- ◆ Cocktails, caviar
- ◆ Fois gras, toast
- ◆ Rainbow trout
- ◆ Vichyssoise soup, rolls
- ◆ Trout en gelee, watercress rolls
- ◆ Roast pheasant
- ◆ Braised celery, bread sauce, gravy
- ◆ Alpine grotto
- ◆ Coffee, liquors

Weekend in Santa Cruz, October 18, 19, and 20

~

Mr. and Mrs. Sonny Werblin, Mr. and Mrs. Phil Isin.

~

FRIDAY DINNER:

- Cocktails, caviar, pâté de fois gras
  - Mushroom soup
  - Fillet of sole
  - Alumette potatoes
  - Artichokes
- Caramel custard, whipped cream
  - Coffee, liquors

SATURDAY BREAKFAST:

- Orange juice, Danish pastries, coffee

SATURDAY LUNCH:

- Jellied madrilene
- Cold veal, ham pie, cold stripper beef, cold tongue
  - Salad, French bread
  - Raspberries, crème double

SUNDAY DINNER:

- Pâté maison
- Trout meunière, watercress rolls
  - Chicken-on-spit
  - Small sautéed potatoes, peas
  - Duke of Windsor
  - Coffee, liquors

November 10, 1963

~

Dinner for four for Sir Malcom Sargeant (English conductor)
Extra help: Chrystal, Rose

~

MENU:

- Canapes: caviar, cheese rolls
- Mushroom soup, rolls
- Trout meunière, watercress rolls
- Saddle of lamb
- Peas in zucchini, small potatoes, gravy
- Brie cheese, crackers
- Raspberries in pineapple, crème double
- Coffee, liquors

November 16, 1963

~⌒

Dinner for three for Sean Connery.
Extra help: Chrystal

~⌒

MENU:

- Canapes: caviar, vodka, cheese rolls
- Mushroom soup, rolls
- Saddle of lamb
- Peas, small potatoes, mint sauce, gravy
- Brie cheese, crackers
- Raspberry ice cream in pineapple
- Coffee, liquor

Dinner fo Sean Connery's Wife (4). Chrystal & Extra help
December 28th. 1963.

Paté maison
Toast.
(In Cellar).

Celery Soup.
Rolls.

Chicken Supreme.
mushrooms in Patty cases.
Peas.

Raspberries & Ice Cream
in individual Pineapples.

Coffee.

ALMA'S WEEKEND MENUS:

FRIDAY DINNERS

♦ Celery soup
♦ Cheese straws

∾

♦ Poached turbot
♦ Maine parsley potatoes
♦ Hollandaise sauce

∾

♦ Artichokes
♦ Melted butter

∾

♦ Apple flan with whipped cream

∾

WINE: POUILLY FUISSE

or:

♦ String bean soup

∾

♦ Raie au beurre noir
♦ Pommes purée

∾

♦ Caramel custard cream

∾

WINE: POUILLY FUISSE

or:

♦ String bean soup

∾

♦ Sole villette

∾

♦ Raspberries and cream

∾

WINE: CHATEAU HAUT BRION BLANC

SATURDAY BREAKFAST

♦ Coffee   Juice   Danish pastry

SATURDAY LUNCH

- Consomme madrilene (jellied)

~

- Cold steak and kidney pie
- Stripper of beef
- Cold tongue (horseradish)

~

- Peach ice cream Melba

~

WINE: CHATEAU DE SELLE

or:

- Jellied madrilene
- French bread

~

- Cold buffet
- Veal and ham pie
- Stripper
- Tongue
- Salad
- Horseradish sauce

~

- Berries or flan

or:

- Consomme madrilene

~

- Ham
- Sauce Madeira
- Puree of peas
- Maine potatoes

~

- Strawberries
- Double cream

~

WINE: VIN ROSE (PROVENCE)

or:

- Steak en gelée pie

~

- Cold stripper
- Cold tongue with horseradish

+ Salad

~

+ Fruit salad
+ Double cream

SATURDAY DINNERS

+ Lobsters (smoked salmon for Mr. H)
+ Mayonnaise
+ Watercress rolls
+ Salad

~

+ Saddle of lamb
+ Mint sauce

~

+ Boulangère potatoes
+ Peas in squash

~

+ Fresh fruit salad

or:

+ Cold lobster

~

+ Roast fillet (gravy)
+ Bubble and squeak
+ Popovers

~

+ Pickwick

~

WINE: MUSIGNY-MOSELLE

or:

+ Salmon mousse

~

+ Roast veal
+ Stuffing
+ Ham
+ String beans
+ Potatoes

~

+ Fruit salad
+ Cream

⁓

WINE: CHAMBOLLE MUSIGNY
SANCERRE

or:

- Pâté
- Salmon Mousse

⁓

- Chicken on spit
- Small brown potatoes
- Petit pois

⁓

- Hot deep-dish apple and blackberry pie
- Jersey cream

⁓

- Cold raspberry mousse

or:

- Smoked salmon (dark bread and butter)

⁓

- Saddle of lamb with mint sauce
- Peas
- Round squash
- Pommes boulangère
- Gravy

⁓

- Duke of Windsor
- Wild strawberries

⁓

WINE: MUSIGNY

SUNDAY BRUNCHES

- Orange juice   Melon
- Bacon   Sausages
- Kidneys   Mushrooms
- Eggs (not for Hitch)   Popovers

or:

- Crenshaw melon

⁓

- Finnan haddie

⁓

⬧ Apple flan

or:

⬧ Crenshaw melon

～○

⬧ Kidneys
⬧ Sausages
⬧ Eggs (not for Hitch)
⬧ Bacon

～○

⬧ Apple flan
⬧ Cream

or:

⬧ melon

～○

⬧ Quiche Lorraine
⬧ Salad
⬧ Large mushrooms on toast

or:

⬧ Crenshaw melon or cantalope
⬧ Finnan haddie
⬧ Caramel custard

～○

WINE: MUSCADET

SUNDAY DINNERS:

⬧ Pâté in solarium

～○

⬧ Poulet Côte d'Or
⬧ Pois
⬧ Pommes
⬧ Sauce supreme

～○

⬧ Pot de cream

～○

WINE: MONTRACHET

or:

⬧ Pate in patio

～○

⬧ Chickens on spit

♦ Pommes Parisienne
♦ Asparagus tips

∿

♦ Peach flan

or:

♦ Crenshaw melon
or
♦ Mushroom soup

∿

♦ Saddle of lamb
♦ Mint sauce
♦ Roast potatoes
♦ String beans
♦ Squash
♦ Gravy

∿

♦ Coupe Jacques
or
♦ Peach Melba

or:

♦ Pâté
♦ Chicken (lightly roasted)
♦ Sauce supreme

∿

♦ Raspberry souffle

∿

WINE: MONTRACHET

or:

♦ Cold salmon trout with mayonnaise
♦ Watercress rolls

∿

♦ Chicken on spit
♦ Pommes Parisienne
♦ Asparagus tips
♦ Gravy

∿

♦ Fresh fruit salad
♦ Cream

∿

WINE: MONTRACHET

MONDAY LUNCH

- Cold celery soup

∽

- Cold lobster

∽

- Cheese

MONDAY DINNER

- Hot consomme

∽

- Dover soles
- Pommes alumette

∽

- Flan

Bibliography & Resources

Books

Auiler, Dan. *Hitchcock's Notebooks.* New York: Avon Books, Inc., 1999.

Barr, Charles. *English Hitchcock.* Cameron & Hollis, Moffat, 1999.

Bogdanovich, Peter. *Who The Devil Made It.* New York: Alfred A. Knopf, 1997.

Brill, Leslie. *The Hitchcock Romance: Love and Irony in Hitchcock's Films.* Princeton, N.J.: Princeton University Press, 1988.

Condon, Paul & Sangster, Jim. *The Complete Hitchcock.* Virgin Publishing Ltd., 1999.

Dentlebaum and Leland Poague, Eds. *A Hitchcock Reader.* Ames: Iowa State University Press, 1986.

DeRosa, Steven. *Writing with Hitchcock.* New York and London: Faber, 2001.

Durgnat, Raymond. *The Strange Case of Alfred Hitchcock.* Cambridge, Mass.: MIT Press, 1974.

Finler, Joel W., *Hitchcock in Hollywood.* New York: Continuum Publishing Group, 1992.

Freeman, David. *The Last Days of Alfred Hitchcock.* New York: Overlook Press, 1984.

Halley, Michael. *The Alfred Hitchcock Album.* Englewood Cliffs, N.J.: Prentice Hall, 1981.

Harris, Robert A. and Lasky, Michael S. *The Films of Alfred Hitchcock.* New York: Citadel Press, 1976.

Humphries, Patrick. *The Films of Alfred Hitchcock.* Greenwich, Conn.: Brom Books, 1986.

Kapsis, Robert E. *Hitchcock: The Making of a Reputation.* Chicago: University of Chicago Press, 1992.

Krohn, Bill. *Hitchcock Au Travail.* Cahiers du Cinema, 1999.

Leff, Leonard J. *Hitchcock and Selznick.* New York: Weidenfeld & Nicholson, 1987.

Leitch, Thomas M. *Find the Director and Other Hitchcock Games.* Athens: University of Georgia Press, 1991.

———. *The Encyclopedia of Alfred Hitchcock.* New York: Checkmark Books, 2002.

Low, Rachel. *The History of the British Film.* London: George Allen and Unwin, Ltd., 1985.

Maxford, Howard. *The A–Z of Hitchcock.* The Ultimate Reference Guide. London: B.T. Batsford, 2002.

McGillian, Pat. *Backstory: Interviews with Screenwriters of Hollywood's Golden Age.* Berkeley & Los Angeles, London: University of California Press, 1986.

Modelski, Tania. *The Women Who Knew Too Much: Hitchcock and Feminist Theory.* New York: Methuen, 1988.

Park, James. *British Cinema: The Lights That Failed.* London: B.T. Batsford, 1991.

Perry, George. *The Films of Alfred Hitchcock.* New York: Dutton/Vista, 1965.

———. *Hitchcock.* Garden City, N.Y.: Doubleday, 1975.

Phillips, Gene D. *Alfred Hitchcock.* Boston: Twayne Publishing, 1984.

Raubicheck, Walter, and Srebnick, Walter, eds. *Hitchcock's Rereleased Films: From* Rope *to* Vertigo. Wayne, Nebr.: Wayne State University Press, 1991.

Rebello, Stephen. *Alfred Hitchcock and the Making of* Psycho. New York: Dembner Books, 1990.

Rohmer, Eric, and Charbol, Claude. *Hitchcock: The First 44 Films.* New York: Frederick Ungar, 1979.

Rothman, William. *Hitchcock: The Murderous Gaze.* Cambridge, Mass.: Harvard University Press, 1982.

Ryall, Tom. *Alfred Hitchcock and the British Cinema.* Urbana, Ill.: University of Illinois Press, 1986.

Sharff, Stephan. *Alfred Hitchcock's High Vernacular.* New York: Columbia University Press, 1991.

Simone, Sam P. *Hitchcock as Activist: Politics and the War Films.* UMI Research Press, 1985.

Sinyard, Neil. *The Films of Alfred Hitchcock.* New York: Galley Books, 1986.

Smith, Steven C. *A Heart at Fire's Center: The Life and Music of Bernard Herrmann.* Berkeley: University of California Press, 1991.

Spotto, Donald. *The Dark Side of Genius: The Life of Alfred Hitchcock.* Boston: Little, Brown, 1983.

——. *The Art of Alfred Hitchcock: Fifty Years of His Motion Pictures.* New York: Anchor Books, 1992.

Street, Sarah. *British National Cinema.* New York: Routledge, 1997.

Taylor, John Russell. *Hitch: The Life and Times of Alfred Hitchcock.* New York: Pantheon Books, 1978.

Truffaut, François. *Hitchcock/Truffaut.* New York: Simon & Schuster, 1983.

Villien, Bruno. *Hitchcock.* Paris: Rivages, 1985.

Weiss, Elisabeth. *The Silent Scream: Alfred Hitchcock's Soundtrack.* Associated University Press, 1982.

Wood, Robin. *Hitchcock's Films Revisited.* New York: Columbia University Press, 1989.

Yacowar, Maurice. *Hitchcock's British Films.* Hamden, Conn.: Archon Books, 1977.

PERIODICALS

Anonymous. "Lost Treasures of Cinema Unearthed." *The Observer,* September 4, 1995.

Anonymous. "It's In The Bag." *Variety, Hollywood Reporter,* February 8, 1945.

Anonymous. "After The Verdict." *The Film Daily,* January 26, 1930.

Anonymous. "The Blackguard." *Variety,* May 27, 1925.

Anonymous. "The First Born." *Pacific Film Archive,* June 30, 1985.

Anonymous. "Woman to Woman." *Variety,* April 2, 1924.

Anonymous. "The Outsider." *Variety,* April 29, 1931.

Anonymous. "Sally in our Alley." *Variety,* November 2, 1927.

Anonymous. "The Water Gypsies." *Variety,* April 19, 1932.

Anonymous. "Forbidden Territory." *Variety,* November 6, 1934.

Anonymous. "The Passing of the Third Floor Back." *Variety,* May 6, 1936.

Anonymous. "Constant Nymph." *Variety,* March 21, 1928.

Anonymous. Untitled. *New World Illustrated,* April 11, 1940.

Anonymous. "Alma in Wonderland." *The Picturegoer,* December 1925.

Abramson, Martin. "What Hitchcock Does With His Blood Money."

Beckett, Henry. "Pat Never Says 'My Old Man' But Miss Hitchcock Is Quite American." *New York Post*, January 7, 1942.

Benedette, M. "A Day With Hitchcock."

Champlin, Charles. "Alma Reville—The Unsung Partner." *Los Angeles Times*, July 19, 1982.

Davis, Igor. "One Woman Who Has Never Been Frightened By Mr. Hitchcock." *Daily Express*, August 4, 1974.

Heath, Tony. "Lloyd George Movie Found After 76 Years." *The Observer*, London, December 4, 1994.

Hitchcock, Alfred. "The Woman Who Knows Too Much." *McCalls*, March 1956.

Hitchcock, Alma, As Told to Elizabeth Sherrill. *Everyone's Family Circle*, June 1958.

Hitchcock, Alma, as told to Martin Abramson. "My Husband, Alfred Hitchcock, Hates Suspense." *Coronet*, August 1964.

Hitchcock, Patricia, as told to Marya Saunders. "My Dad, The Jokester." *Citizen News*, July 7, 1963.

Kaytor, Marily, Producer. *The Alfred Hitchcock Dinner Hour. Look*, August 27, 1963.

Mannock, P. L. "Two New British Production Units." *Kinematograph Weekly*, October 8, 1925.

McBride, Joseph. "Nothing Will Ever Stop Hitch." *Variety*, October 28, 1975.

———. "Mr. and Mrs. Hitchcock." *Sight and Sound*, Fall 1976.

Reville, Alma, As Told to Elizabeth Sherrill. "My Husband Hates Suspense." *Everyone's Family Cicrle*, June 1958.

Russell Taylor, John. "Alma Hitchcock." *Take One*, May 1976.

Thomas, Kevin. "Griffith Film Still Stunning." *Los Angeles Times*, January 23, 1976.

Vincent, Sally. "When the Master of Suspense Bolts His Own Door At Night." *Daily Express*, June 8, 1960.

Warwick, Alan. "Alfred Hitchcock's Tudor Cottage." *Home Chat*, February 27, 1932.

Weston Edwards, Joan. "Making Good in the Film Trade." February 26, 1927.

PERMISSIONS

Photo on title page copyright © 1976 Universal Pictures.

Photo on page 11 copyright © 1942 Universal Pictures Company, Inc.

Photo on page 172 copyright © 1955 Samuel Taylor and
Patricia Hitchcock O'Connell as trustees under the second
will of Alfred Hitchcock.

Photos on page 191 copyright © 1963 Alfred J. Hitchcock
Productions, Inc.

Photo on page 201 copyright © 1972 Universal Pictures Limited.

Photo on page 208 copyright © 1966 Universal Pictures.

Photo on page 215 copyright © 1976 Universal Pictures.

Photo on page 217 copyright © 1976 Universal Pictures.

Photo on page 223 copyright © 1964 Geoffrey Stanley, Inc.

All other photos courtesy of Hitchcock Family Collection.